BEATRIZ COSTA   TIAGO FRANCO
ILLUSTRATIONS BY MARIA GRILO

Product Design Process

**The manual for digital product
design and project management.**

Visit our website at www.imaginarycloud.com

Design and illustrations by Maria Grilo

Editorial coordination by Sandro Cantante

Editorial revision by Gavin King

First paperback edition May 2019

ISBN: 9-789871-973644

Printed in the United States of America by IngramSpark

Tiago Franco's acknowledgements:

This book is the culmination of almost a decade of hard work. The Product Design Process was developed with the help and input of many industry professionals and clients, that participated in a couple hundred projects at Imaginary Cloud. The book would have not been possible without them. We're very grateful for all their dedication and hope they feel well represented in these pages.

Beatriz Costa acknowledgements:

I would like to acknowledge Nicholas Mandelbaum, that in his passage by Imaginary Cloud put together a first sequence of selected design deliveries and helped me to become a better product designer thanks to his guidance and feedback.

Index

CHAPTER 1

Introduction

Product design is gradually becoming harder to define. What once consisted of simply providing a solution to a specific problem through a material product has evolved into a host of different solutions, platforms and variations on the same theme. The design thinking behind product development has given way to multiple paths with the same end-goal, each leading to multiple fields of knowledge, distinct skill sets, and various techniques. Concepts such as User Experience (UX) and User Interface (UI) are now more widely used and represent a shift from the old paradigm. It is critical to know who will be using the product and not just what problem it is meant to solve because understanding the user has become as important as perceiving the problem and providing the solution. In order to answer the many challenges of designing a web product, several techniques have been developed and applied in recent years. Most of them are merely different variations on the same approach while others are better suited to certain phases of the product lifecycle. However, there is no single technique that is sufficient on its own and there is no main technique that should be used to the exclusion of others.

This multiplicity of available options gives product design teams more freedom to pick what suits them best but also creates uncertainty regarding which tools and techniques should be used for each problem. Therefore, when a product design team takes on a new project, there is usually a set of questions for which they seek satisfying answers:

- Which techniques are needed to develop a product?
- Which techniques best complement each other?
- In terms of schedule, which tasks can be developed at the same time?
- Which dependencies exist amongst the various techniques?
- How can the output generated by one technique be used as an input for the next step in order to guarantee that the resulting progress is reflected in the final product and adds value to it?

To address those questions, Imaginary Cloud developed the Product Design Process (PDP), a collection of existing techniques, matured over time by the industry and chained together to ensure that the product design team's workflow is as efficient as possible. It was developed over the last eight years based on field experience and, during this period, has been applied to hundreds of digital products by design and development professionals, improving through the feedback provided by real world experience in a range of contexts. What began as a design thinking sprint with a vaguely defined objective resulted in a well-structured and optimized process only possible by the contributions of many professionals and through the creation of numerous iterations. In the last three years, the structure of the process has achieved stability, signaling that it has reached a maturity level suitable for industry adoption.

This process has the following advantages when compared to lighter design processes or unstructured approaches:

• Reduced design and development time (and costs) by avoiding excessive feedback loops with change requests;

• Predictability enabling the planning of realistic schedules;

• Improved expectations management, resulting in less stress for the product owner and team members;

• A higher quality final product;

• Happier product owners.

PDP has a number of features that support the listed advantages. First, all design decisions are based on research or clearly identified assumptions shared by the whole team. Second, the product owner has close involvement and enhanced visibility of the reasoning that leads to design decisions. Third, the product design plan is well structured and every member of the team knows what to expect from each phase.

Who should read this manual?

This book is useful for anyone involved in the design or development of digital products, providing an accessible overview of the design process, the detail of its phases, and the respective tasks. Despite being suitable for everyone that participates in the development lifecycle of a digital product, the book is particularly relevant for the following audiences:

• UX/UI design practitioners that want to improve the efficiency of their creative process;

09

• Leaders of UX design groups seeking better ways to articulate and coordinate the various UX/UI tasks and techniques;

• Leaders of product development teams that want to understand the resources, techniques, and tools needed for product design as well as the dependencies between these elements;

• Product owners that wish to have a clearer view into the effort and tasks that sit at the heart of product design;

• Product developers that seek to broaden their knowledge of the product design process in order to improve the development of their UX/UI implementations.

Where will we focus?

One of the benefits of PDP is its selection of techniques indispensable to the success of any product design and their efficient articulation, allowing a lean approach with a continuous and fluid progression of product development. This manual does not present an exhaustive list of all the existing UX techniques nor does it pretend to be a rigid and universal formula. Its focus is on the process and how the presented techniques work together. The execution of each of them requires some technical knowledge, which the reader is presumed to already possess. The reader does not need to be a highly experienced product owner, designer, or developer in order to fully understand this book but some previous experience in product design is required, so that when we discuss concepts like Wireframes and Prototypes, the reader understands what we are referring to. Knowledge of more advanced topics like executing user interview sessions, knowledge of Information Architecture[1], Heuristic Evaluation (developed by Jakob Nielsen and Rolf Molich), Gestalt Principles[2] and Color Theory would also be beneficial to the reader. Software developers should also be familiar with the design of software architecture and its planning (either Agile or Waterfall will do, as PDP is suited to both approaches).

Although this is a stable process we are conscious that new techniques and tools will continue to appear. Some of these might result in significant improvements to our process and, once it happens, updates to PDP will be released in new editions of this book.

References

1. Information Architects (Richard Saul Wurman, 1996)
2. Principles of Gestalt Psychology (Kurt Koffka, 1935)

11

CHAPTER 2

Overview

PDP is a user centered design process for digital products and it follows a multi-disciplinary approach that places emphasis on co-creation by product owners and specialized professionals. Its overarching goal is the design of world-class digital products with a fast go-to-market strategy but it can also be applied to projects that seek product growth through optimization.

The team that takes part in PDP must be composed of people with competences in the following five disciplines: product management, user research, visual design, software architecture design, and project planning. At Imaginary Cloud we give preference to teams consisting of a product owner, a UX designer, a UI designer and an experienced CTO. This arrangement usually performs better than other team configurations that we have tried but, despite our own experience, different contexts may require other approaches. Thus it is possible that your ideal configuration differs from ours. However, independently of the team configuration, make sure that each of the five competencies is represented by people that have actual experience in the required areas. When possible, avoid assigning user research and visual design tasks to a single team member as, despite both falling under the design umbrella, they consist of distinct disciplines that demand specific training and rely on different knowledge (for instance, sociology and cognitive psychology for user research and plastic arts and illustration for visual design). Although the process requires a diverse set of skills, the team should be pragmatic and only use the resources necessary for each step. It is critical to resist the temptation of involving everyone in each step and ensure that only those who have the required knowledge or possess the necessary skills participate at relevant points.

The Product Design Process consists of four phases: Research, Ideation, Execution, and Technical Assessment. Each phase is then split into several steps.

An overview of the Product Design Process can be seen in Figure 1, showing three phases on the left side of the arrow and one on the right. The first phase – Research – is shown on the top left side. This early stage is the UX designer's responsibility and its objective is to gather, from the product owner and potential users, evidence that will support the decisions taken henceforth, thus ensuring that no decision is made based on vague assumptions. This is where the main aspects of the business model and user needs are identified. The second phase is Ideation. This is the core of the creative process and hence where the concept of the product is formulated based on the users' needs and the business model, both identified in the Research phase. At this phase, the UX designer, the visual designer and the product owner should work closely together. The third phase is Execution and

Research

1. Briefing
2. User Research
3. Design Benchmark

Technical Assessment

11. High-level Architecture
12. Project Plan

Ideation

4. User Journey
5. Decision Matrix
6. Wireframes
7. Mood Board

Execution

8. Style Guide
9. Graphic User Interface Design
10. Prototype

Figure 1/ The Product Design Process, organized by phases and steps

it is the last one on the left side of Figure 1. It is the visual designer's responsibility and focuses on creating a physical representation of the concept that has been defined up to this point. The phase on the right side, Technical Assessment, is a responsibility of the CTO. The objective is to guarantee that all requirements and ideas generated are realistic concerning their implementation and achievable given the available time and budget.

The four phases follow a sequence that should be respected, as the outputs generated by steps in the previous phases are a requirement to the steps in the phases that follow. It is a common practice in design to develop several tasks at the same time. However, this practice can be more harmful than efficient. It is impossible to generate good ideas without understanding the problem that the team is trying to solve, and execution is infeasible without understanding what needs to be built. Every time a new idea is prototyped on top of immature requirements, substantial parts of the work already done in past iterations will have to be rethought out and redesigned, forcing a complete rework of the prototype or resulting in a product that will look patched together instead of built as an integrated whole. Consequently, the primary results of executing several steps without a specific logical order is the higher cost (in time and resources) as well as the eventual loss of motivation because the team will have to rework the product again with increased pressure. If there is need to build on a product, the right way to do it is to revisit the previous phases. For instance, if new feedback needs to be incorporated in a Prototype, the team should revisit and baseline the previous phases before completing the needed changes. Regarding the fourth phase, the Technical Assessment, although most of the work done at this

16

phase is usually executed near the end of PDP, the CTO will need to be in constant communication with designers. It is important to have a technical team member who is able to jump in and clarify if the implementation costs and effort of a given solution will meet the constraints of the project's budget and defined schedule, or if an alternative solution needs to be found.

A critical requirement for the success of PDP is the constant communication with the product owner that allows short cycles of feedback and, thus, short execution times. Throughout the process, in each step, there should be at least three points of communication: first, an initial workshop; second a status update when the execution of each step is at its midpoint; third and finally meeting to validate every step. However, in between checkpoints it is important for the team to focus on each step to be completed without any additional input that may cause unnecessary diversions. At each meeting, the team should always have additional value to contribute and for which to gather feedback. Following the same idea, if the product owner is not available for the midpoint status update the team should initiate the remaining steps of the phase to avoid project delays.

Inside each phase you can find several steps that can be done at the same time. This allows you to accommodate for different project characteristics, team members' preferences and even the availability of the product owner, without compromising the product quality or the project time frame and budget. Table 1, on the next page, presents the various steps in each phase, providing a description for each one and summarizing its objectives.

17

PHASE	STEP	DESCRIPTION
1 / RESEARCH	**Briefing**	• Workshop with the team (usually one to four hours) to present the vision and the goals of the project and clarify all necessary business requirements. Assures that the whole team is working on the same page and with all the relevant information to start the project.
	User Research	• Explore the user profiles with the product stakeholders; • Define target user profiles (Personas), clearly identifying the users' motivations and goals for using the product. Guarantees product usefulness and effectiveness from the users' point of view.
	Design Benchmark	• Research the landscape of similar and complementary products; • Analyse design patterns and technologies used in the industry and on similar activities; • Position the new product in this landscape. This allows us to leverage the knowledge and skills of existing players and assure feature/design differentiation.
2 / IDEATION	**User Journey**	• Map the ideal user experience, describing the main steps performed by the user; • Write and validate the user scenarios. Provides a vision of the global user experience, ensuring its consistency and fluidity. Serves as a base to establish the product requirements.
	Decision Matrix	• List and prioritise the user stories; • Prioritise taking into account the user goals, the product goals and the current stage of the product lifecycle. Provides an indispensable basis for the project development plan ensuring that, even under time and cost constraints, a viable product can be developed.
	Wireframes	• Draw the skeleton of the screens covered by PDP, defining the pages structure and navigation flow. Improves interface usability and reduces design time by baselining the core information architecture.

PHASE	STEP	DESCRIPTION
3 / EXECUTION ⋮	**Mood Board**	• Scout the product's "mood" through a collection of pictures, words, and other visual elements. Assures that the product's look & feel conveys the desired user experience and is aligned with the user profile and market strategy.
	Style Guide	• Baseline the graphic interface styling: color palette, fonts, image style, input fields, buttons and other page elements. Assures the consistency throughout the application, baselining the visual coherence of different graphic interface elements.
	Graphic User Interface Design	• Execute the end-looking screens by applying the Style Guide to the Wireframes. Provides stakeholders with the final aspect of the product's screens in order to obtain approval before moving to the implementation.
	Prototype	• Develop a click-through Prototype, accessible online and shareable with other devices and users through a link and password. Allows the navigation from screen-to-screen, facilitating the feedback intake either from stakeholders or from potential users and investors.
4 / TECHNICAL ASSESSMENT	**High-level Architecture**	• Develop the technical design with the ideal balance between complexity and reach; • Identify the external dependencies from third party providers (e.g. Stripe, Facebook, Amazon). Details how the product is going to be built, identifying baselines for the needed technologies and skills to build it.
	Project Plan	• Define the major milestones, providing a general understanding of the project's structure, phases, intersections and interdependencies. Allows a good understanding of how to build the product, how much effort it will require and the expected costs for each product phase.

Once PDP is completed and the first version is launched, it is important to improve on the product following a design/build/learn cycle. However, these post-launch changes are usually different from the ones that were identified during the development of the first prototype. They usually consist of small details derived from the users' feedback that have a low risk of compromising the existing Graphic User Interface (GUI), improving upon a solid base that has already been defined through PDP. Post-launch changes occur with less frequency during the lifespan of the product and are usually less critical to the business. At this stage the product is already in a testing phase or even live and it is not necessary to quickly have a version ready for feedback.

We have written this manual to share what we consider to be a successful Product Design Process. However, we have also invested great effort in making this a practical manual that could be used as a field guide during the planning and execution of PDP. To provide a thorough and structured view of PDP we have given each of the processes' steps its own chapter. For every step, you will find a short introduction and an answer to the questions "why", "what", "how", followed by a practical example. The first of these sections is dedicated to an explanation of why that step is important by itself and as part of the process, and will contemplate the concepts and goals that will later be explained and achieved, respectively. On the second section, we describe what the step is objectively, as well as other concepts that may be important in its context. The "how" section is focused on the methodology in itself, and it is where we will provide the way in which the goals mentioned before are going to be achieved. Each chapter then concludes with a practical example that illustrates the step's concepts and instructions on how to achieve the expected outcome.

20

CHAPTER 3

Briefing

The Briefing is the first step of the actual PDP. Before it, you should however, have already done the formal project kick-off. That way, when you start PDP all the team members are familiar with each other and with any potentially challenging social dynamic, so an effective communication can be established during the course of the process. Here at the Briefing the main goal is to guarantee that all team members share the existing knowledge relevant to the product design.

Why

Usually, when the design process starts, the product owner already has thought about the desired product. In some cases, there is only a vague idea, in others there is already a detailed vision of what the product should be. Both scenarios place specific challenges. For example, a product owner that only has a vague notion of the desired product might require special attention in the creative User Journey and Mood Board steps, in order to explore the possible paths before picking a direction. By contrast, if the product owner has a more detailed vision of the desired result it probably means that there was already considerable time and effort invested in the concept making it harder to break pre-existing beliefs. Given the possible lack of design knowledge, such beliefs could be problematic as they might be based on unjustifiable assumptions. In these cases, special consideration should be given to the User Research and Design Benchmark steps in order to carefully deconstruct unfit ideas with solid data while not compromising relations between the product owner and the rest of the product design team. In both cases, however, at this stage the product owner has knowledge about the product that the technical team does not yet have and it is crucial to manage the client expectations and design a good solution accordingly.

24

What

The Briefing consists of a workshop with, at minimum, the product owner and the UX design team member in attendance, and it can be done both presencially or by remote conference. It usually lasts from one to four hours but on very complex products it could take some days to complete. The duration and number of sessions depends on the type of product, the maturity of the idea, the profile of the team members, or even on the communication style (for instance, in some cases the communication focuses on pragmatic information, while in others, it is similar to a storytelling style).

How

When the Briefing starts, as we have seen before, the product owner has already some information about the product and its industry. The role of the UX designer at this stage is to make all the necessary questions to understand all the existing client requirements as well as all the knowledge relevant to understand the product context. The discussion will vary depending mainly on the maturity of the product idea, as well as the type of product.

If the product owner does not have a detailed set of ideas for the product, the Briefing will be a short meeting consisting of the concept definition being done in the follow-on steps. If the product owner already has articulated requirements, it may be necessary to deconstruct those all the way to their foundations. This task is crucial since frequently the product owner's request does not correspond to a particular user need, but refers instead to a way of satisfying that need, which might not be the best one for the given challenge. Good design work involves adopting a critical attitude towards the requirements provided by the product owner and trying to understand the motivations behind them. That way, it is possible to find alternative ways of achieving the same goals and, ideally, these should be user friendly and result in lower implementation and maintenance costs. The outcome of this discussion will be essential to guide the Benchmark.

Regarding the type of product, if you are working with technical specialized software (for instance, healthcare software) the designers will need to acquire knowledge about the regulatory context, as well as specific terminology, processes and formulas. The Briefing is the right moment for the designer to ask the product owner to present any documentation or references needed to understand all

25

business requirements. Then, the UX designer should take its time to carefully go through the documentation individually and get back to the product owner later on to clarify any doubt. However, if you are working on a less specialized market (mass market entertainment, for instance), this step may be skipped.

Lastly, a crucial information you want to take from the Briefing is which target users the product owner has in mind. While the actual users' profiles will be defined in the next step, the User Research, it is important to know at who you should start looking at so you can recruit people to user interviews or have a basis for writing your proto-personas, a concept that will be covered in the following steps.

Examples

Imagine that the idea consists on a market place and that one of the requirements that the client communicates is the need to have in the homepage a call to action button that redirects the user to a signup process. When asking why does the product owner wants to direct the users from the homepage to the signup process, you may discover that it is because they want to collect emails from the users. You can then, during PDP, look into alternative ways to achieve their goal (it could be, for instance, a simple newsletter subscription field, since this is an option that requires less time and effort from the user). However, the product owner goal may be to direct the users to the signup as a first step to the purchase. You may want then, at the Benchmark phase, to look into alternative checkout flows that require minimum user input.

27

Further Reading

A Project Guide to UX Design: For user experience designers in the field or in the making (Ross Unger and Carolyn Chandler, 2009)

CHAPTER 4

User Research

There are many techniques available to facilitate User Research and each of them has a particular use to analyze and evaluate different dimensions of usability. Ideally, a design process should include User Research at different moments. However, due to time and budget constraints it is oftentimes necessary to account for the cost-benefit tradeoff and go with only one moment of user research before the product launch. The positioning of the User Research at the start of the process is the option that allows a more significant risk reduction. It guarantees that the product requirements are based on data rather than on assumptions, thus assuring that the product is successful in the most fundamental dimension of usability: usefulness[1]. Additionaly, it guarantees that further iterations in the product will be only at the level of the interface details and not at the level of the product concept and its functional requirements.

In the Product Design Process, we have a preference for the Persona technique over other methods. This method has been chosen because of its exploratory nature, making it suited for early phases of the design process, and its straightforward structure that facilitates the organization and summarization of qualitative information (which, as opposed to quantitative information, gives us rich insights and does not need a large number of users to be insightful).

Why

In UX design there are many perspectives on the role and potential of the Persona method. Some professionals see it as a technique focused mainly – if not exclusively – on the creation of empathy between the users and the product development team while others claim that the Persona method may harm the product because it is based on stereotypes and assumptions.

However, when used properly, Personas have vast potential as a crucial base on which to establish a product's requirements and thus ensure its usefulness. Since this is done in the early stages of the process, it can drastically reduce the project's risks. It can also help the team avoid wasting resources developing a concept for which the user would see little utility and also prevents some common project mistakes. There are three main risks that Personas allow us to avoid: the elastic user, self-referential design, and edge cases[2]:

• The elastic user: Everyone on a product team has their own ideas about who the user is and what the user needs. When the time to make product decisions comes, this "user" becomes elastic, conveniently bending and stretching to fit the opinions and assumptions of whoever is contributing.

• Self-referential design: when designers or developers project their own views and biases onto the process and its results.

• Edge cases: design for edge cases – situations that could occur but that are unlikely for most people. Typically, edge cases must be designed and built for, but they should never be the design focus.

What

Personas are simple written documents that describe fictional (but realistic) characters that model – existing and potential – product users. Though conceptually straightforward, the way in which Personas are executed varies greatly in the variety and quantity of the information that they contain and these factors are critical to the value that this method may add to, or detract from, the design process.

In PDP we follow the Goal Oriented Persona methodology[2]. Following this approach, each Persona is constructed with demographic information, a context, goals, frustrations, and behaviors. What distinguishes the Goal Oriented Persona from other approaches is its relegation of demographic information and the user context to a secondary level and its focus on goals and needs.

31

How

There is a simple process that must be followed to build a Persona that represents your target user. The objective at the end of the User Research step is to have a clear idea of who you are addressing with your product and which problems you are looking to provide an answer to. In this section, we will cover in depth each stage in the process of building a realistic Persona - collecting information, compiling information, building the profiles, and prioritizing the profiles.

COLLECTING INFORMATION

There are several ways to collect the information on which Personas are based. In an ideal scenario, where there is the necessary time and budget, user interviews should be a rule of thumb. This technique allows the gathering of the qualitative information needed and it is less time and cost consuming in comparison to other techniques such as contextual inquires. If you do not have the time or budget for interviewing users, you can, however, base your Personas on the product owner's existing knowledge about the them. In that case, you will be constructing what is known as proto-personas. These allow you to avoid the common pitfalls (elastic user, self-referential design, and edge cases) by allowing you to baseline assumptions, but it is important to be aware of the risks that can result from this type of Persona. If the assumptions are proven to be wrong after the product launch, it highly compromises its success in achieving the desired goals.

32

COMPILING INFORMATION

Once the qualitative information is gathered it is time to develop the Personas. You should create a maximum of three Personas per graphic interface (if the product consists of various interfaces, there should be a maximum of three for each). Frequently, the temptation exists to create more Personas, but these are usually redundant or even harmful because of the conflicting needs of different users and, even if they are not contradictory, "when you broadly design and arbitrarily extend a product's functionality to include many constituencies, you increase the cognitive load and navigational overhead of all users" (2).

As mentioned before, Personas should not correspond to a single interviewed person, but to a mixture of data gathered from several individuals with the same end-goals. If a Persona matches one person, you will end up with a limited vision of who you are addressing, creating too rigid of a profile. In reality, even if target users are people with the same goals, they are probably very different in many respects. This way, when moving from the interviews to the Persona creation, the first step is to group profiles of individuals that have the same end goals. You should then observe how the experience, goals, and other attributes relevant to the project's context, such as personality traits, the degree of familiarity with technology, or the level of expertise differ from group to group. If there is not a significant variance, you are not looking at different Personas, but at one Persona with various end goals.

In PDP we use two simple rules to define Personas in a systematic way thus avoiding the creation of various redundant Personas that will only create noise in the process:

- Each Persona attribute must be graded, rating its impact as none, low, medium, high or very high;
- Comparing any pair of Personas, at a minimum 60% of their attributes should be scored differently. For instance, if you have ten attributes defined, when comparing any pair of Personas, they should have at least six attributes that are scored differently.

BUILDING PERSONAS

Each Persona should consist of demographic information, user context, goals, needs, frustrations and behaviors.

- Demographic Information: The Persona should have a very limited amount of demographic characteristics, consisting only of attributes necessary to make it a realistic character that will contain the relevant information covered further ahead. Also, they should not be the criteria to develop Personas, but only be added after the Personas are established as randomly as possible, avoiding the creation of stereotypes. "Do not confuse Persona archetypes with stereotypes. Stereotypes are, in most respects, the antithesis of well-developed Personas"[2].

- User Context: The Persona should have both a quote and some background story to increase its perceived humanity. The quote should be a short phrase that captures its essence, in the context of the product being developed and so that it is possible to tell the Personas apart by each related quote. The background story should be kept short in order to not lose the focus on goals.

- Goals: As it was already mentioned, goals are the core of Personas and they can be defined as "the drivers behind behaviors"[2]. It is important to distinguish them apart from other three concepts with which goals are usually confused: strategies, tasks, and actions. Personas should only include goals and not strategies (and definitely not tasks or actions) because a strategy does not tell us what the person really wants and it is simply one set of means to reach a goal among other possible approaches. If you assume a specific strategy from the start, which usually consists on the first thing that comes to mind, you are not allowing space for innovation and creativity. There may be other strategies that provide a better answer to the user's needs and that could result in lower development costs. Consequently, strategies should be left out of the Research phase. For a better reference, Table 2 provides a summary of the differences between goals, strategies, tasks and actions.

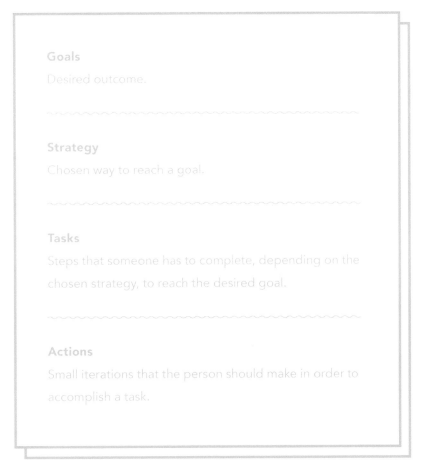

Goals
Desired outcome.

Strategy
Chosen way to reach a goal.

Tasks
Steps that someone has to complete, depending on the chosen strategy, to reach the desired goal.

Actions
Small iterations that the person should make in order to accomplish a task.

Table 2/ Difference between goals, stategy, tasks and actions

Equally important is a set of goal types that will play an important part in the following steps albeit each in a different way. Life goals are important to provide an overall picture that establishes a relationship with the Persona; end goals are used in the Decision Matrix and User Journey steps, helping the designer to make better decisions; experience goals, while also important for the User Journey, will play the biggest part in the Mood Board, as they represent the subjective experience that will define the mood, tone, and communication style. In Table 3, we will specify and define each goal type in more detail:

• Needs and Frustrations: This section seeks to identify the needs that, in the product's context, the user wants to see addressed or the problems that arise when trying to satisfy the user's needs.

• Behaviors: This is where we can find a description of the Persona's behavior in the context of the product's usage (in the event that the product already has an implemented version) or in another similar product context. It is important to focus on the current users' behaviors and not extrapolate to several hypothetical scenarios of how the user could interact with the product. Apart from behavior in the digital product usage context, you should also include behaviors outside of the digital sphere that could in any way relate to the product or its usage in the personal context of the Persona. Exactly which behaviors are relevant is dependent on the product under development, but it is important to define each behavior's frequency and volume. Frequency is the number of times that the Persona engages in a behavior and volume concerns what the Persona gains from it.

36

Life goals

"Personal aspirations that typically go beyond the context of the product being designed. These goals represent deep drivers and motivations that help explain why the user is trying to accomplish the end goal. Life goals describe a person's long-term desires, motivations, and self-image attributes."

~~~~~~

End Goals

"The user's motivation for performing the tasks associated with using a specific product (…) these goals are the focus of a product's interaction design and information architecture. End goals should be amongst the most significant factors in determining the overall product experience. End goals must be met for users to think that a product is worth their time and money."

~~~~~~

Experience Goals

How someone wants to feel when using the product, or the quality of his or her interaction with the product. These goals provide a focus for a product's visual characteristics, interactions and micro-interactions' feel.

Table 3/ The various types of goals

Once the Personas have been constructed, the final step is to prioritize them. In PDP we establish three priority levels displayed in Table 4: main Persona, secondary Persona and supplemental Persona.

This prioritization is fundamental, as trying to equally address all Personas will result in a disjointed interface, compromising the user experience. Additionally, this hierarchy will be very useful in the Decision Matrix stage because it provides a first step towards the prioritization of the product features.

Features that address the end goals of the main Persona should be priorities for implementation, while those that address only the objectives of the secondary or supplemental Personas may be left until a later phase in the product development cycle.

Main persona

The main target of interface design. This Persona should have its needs fully addressed by the product.

~~~~~~

Secondary persona

It is mostly satisfied by the interface designed for the primary Persona but has some additional needs that can be accommodated later without upsetting the product's ability to serve the primary Persona.

~~~~~~

Supplemental persona

Some of its needs can be answered by using the product, but a few of them will not be addressed by the interface since doing so would compromise the experience of the primary Persona.

39

Table 4/ Persona hierarchy

Examples

As we have already identified the usage of demographic data as one of the most common mistakes in Persona Execution, we will provide some practical examples concerning that specific question.

Regarding the demographics variables, in the context of an app for babysitters, for instance, the tendency would be to think about the female genre as a Persona's demographic aspect. However, assumptions and stereotypes apart, that aspect is completely irrelevant. What matters are which goals the babysitters want to fulfill and what the desired experience is. Accordingly, this variable should be randomly generated or removed at all from the Persona. The assumption of why this is relevant is based on the idea that it determines other characteristics, such as the experience goals. However, that is not necessarily true. Instead of assuming a causality effect, you should simply specify the other characteristics, brushing away the idea that these are consequences of demographic information.

On the next page you can find an example of a deliverable that could be generated from this step, highlighting the persona's characteristics that can impact the relevancy of each profile, without focusing on any demographic aspect.

References

1. Handbook of usability testing: How to plan, design, and conduct effective tests (Jeffrey Rubin and Dana Chisnell, 2008)
2. About face 3: The essentials of interaction design (Alan Cooper, Robert Reimann and David Cronin, 2007)

Further Reading

A project guide to UX design: For user experience designers in the field or in the making (Russ Unger and Carolyn Chandler, 2009)
Interviewing Users: How to Uncover Compelling Insights (Steve Portigal, 2013)

Persona's Profile's Overview

Part Timer

Tech Savvy

Weekly Hours Load

Number of Clients

Specialized Knowledge

Mobile usage

Professional

Tech Savvy

Weekly Hours Load

Number of Clients

Specialized Knowledge

Mobile usage

Exclusive

Tech Savvy

Weekly Hours Load

Number of Clients

Specialized Knowledge

Mobile usage

Professional

"Teaching and helping to raise children is my passion."

BACKGROUND STORY

LIFE GOALS   END GOALS   EXPERIENCE GOALS

FRUSTRATIONS   ONLINE ACTIVITIES   OFFLINE ACTIVITIES

41

Persona's Experience Goals Overview

HUMAN FOCUS   MINIMALISTIC

QUICK
USAGE

TASK
FOCUS

DETAILED   CUSTOMIZABLE

 Part Timer   Professional   Exclusive

CHAPTER 5

Design Benchmark

A product does not exist in a vacuum. It inhabits an ecosystem shared with other products that have already established their position and that influence the user's expectations and behaviors. These can be competitors or simply products that, having different functionalities, happen to be used by the same target audience.

For a new product to succeed, it is imperative to follow market best practices and differentiate them from other existing products. We need to analyze the landscape and the characteristics of products similar to the one being developed in order to understand if there is space in the market for a new entry, what is the potential for innovation, and how the product should be presented.

Why

One of the objectives of the Design Benchmark is to understand the minimum quality standard expected by users and which of their needs, identified in the previous step, are not yet being satisfied through available products. This information is important for the Decision Matrix, helping to establish the minimum functionality that your product must offer and what features should be highlighted

Another of the Benchmark's goals is to analyze how existing products position themselves in terms of business goals and communication style[1]. For this purpose, you should seek to understand during this step how these existing products are addressing users and which communication strategies might have an impact. This information will be important for the Mood Board and for the copy – the textual elements of each page that should ideally be developed during the Wireframes and/or during the GUI Design.

Lastly, the Design Benchmark identifies the interacting structures and GUI of existing products thus providing options for solving eventual iteration, navigation, and hierarchy conflicts. By studying existing solutions, you can avoid losing time reinventing the wheel in the Wireframes and GUI Design steps, improving product usability, and by using standards with which the user is already familiar, you are creating a more intuitive UX.

What

The Design Benchmark consists of a document that compiles and summarizes the functionality offered by existing products that operate in the same market, their value positioning and communication style and their information and iteration display patterns. These should be represented with images, annotations and graphics.

How

The first task in the Design Benchmark is to identify which products you are going to evaluate. To start your list, begin by asking the product owner to identify the main competitors and fill in the gaps by doing your own research on the different channels where the product is going to be available.

Usually, product owners are reluctant in recognizing other products as competitors, highlighting the innovative character of their own ideas and considering only those products with the exact same functionality. However, by the reasons explained before, it is important to do comprehensive research in order to have a Design Benchmark that will add value to the process by providing creative solutions and inspiration. There are four types of products that should be given special attention:

• Products that offer functionalities similar to the ones that your product offers or, in other words, direct competitors (even though the specific features are not yet defined, there should already be a high-level vision of what the product will offer);

• Those that, even if they do not provide the same features, target the same end user goals. This could even include products that are not digital solutions and/or constitute indirect competition;

• Products that address different end goals but target the same users or are part of the same market;

• Other products that belong to different markets, offering different features and addressing other segments of the population but deal with amounts of data or data type similar to what is expected of your product.

Once the list of products is completed, it should be analyzed taking into account three considerations:

45

• Available features;

• Positioning in terms of value and communication style;

• Information and iteration display patterns.

To analyze the provided functionality, you should check those products that were identified as direct competitors. Begin by browsing through each product's website, their descriptions in the various app stores and, whenever possible, try them out. Instead of making an exhaustive list of offered features, try to understand which ones are common amongst the analyzed products and which ones are unique. Equally important is to understand which features are being highlighted in the product communication. Through this analysis, we will have a clear idea of each product's positioning in terms of value and communication styles.

Regarding the communication style, you should also analyze the products that are present in the same market (direct competitors or not) and observe both their interfaces and the platforms on which there are being promoted. Below are some of the questions that you should ask:

• Which colors, typefaces, forms and visual compositions these products use for branding or interface?

• How much content do they provide in the product's presentation and interface?

• Which type of content is used? Media, textual information, or raw data?

• What language style do they use: formal or informal? Technical or familiar? Affirmative or cautious?

• What types of imagery do they use? Photos and illustrations? What is their style: realistic or creative? Formal or familiar? Detailed or minimalist?

Lastly, to analyze the information display patterns you should look at a set of products that deal with similar quantities of data and scan through their layout, navigation and information display, raising questions such as:

• What type of navigation is being used?

• How do they deal with reduced/large amounts of data in order to create an appealing layout?

• How do they handle the idea of linear or flexible processes?

At this point, it is important to involve someone from the development side to evaluate the implementation effort of the various possible GUI approaches for the same situation. This information makes it possible to pick the GUI solutions that, apart from addressing the users' needs, also require the least implementation effort.

The amount of information gathered in the Design Benchmark research might be very extensive. In order to easily derive conclusions that may be applied to the following steps of PDP, it is important to have a visual support that presents a summary of that research containing the GUI as well as the interactions and communication strategies. You may compile various print screens of the product's pages and interfaces and write down notes and highlights along with them. Regarding positioning, in terms of values, you can establish two opposing pairs of characteristics and make a cartesian graphic, representing the direct and indirect competitors. This way, you can rapidly identify the existing space in the market for our product. In the Examples section we'll show how this information can be presented.

47

Examples

Imagine that you are developing a product to manage and archive the users' personal medical history. Regarding the direct competitors, you should be making the following questions: which additional features are they offering? Are they presenting medical information in an exhaustive way or only summaries and alerts in case a problem comes up? Are they designed for the average patient or chronically ill patients? Are they more focused in preventive care information or in monitoring of existing conditions?

Indirect competitors could include other products and services that allow file storing. These might include options such as cloud services, an operative system or even physical products such as dossiers and archivers. It is also important to analyze the way in which all of these organize information such as, for instance, chronologically, alphabetically or by specialty, and the various ways in which it is presented: if through digitalized images, photocopies, summary tables, timelines, graphics, and the like.

Lastly, you could analyze other products, services and materials in the medical industry including posters, health issue awareness websites or other specific medical applications to understand how those materials communicate with the public and which concepts or values they transmit. Two main aspects are relevant: if the materials focus on the professionalism and scientific rigor or on the human factor and empathy and what language is being used, whether technical or familiar. All the information gathered through this research of competitor products should be organized in a way similar to what can be seen at the left side of Figure 3, in which each block will represent commented print-screens from the analyzed solutions.

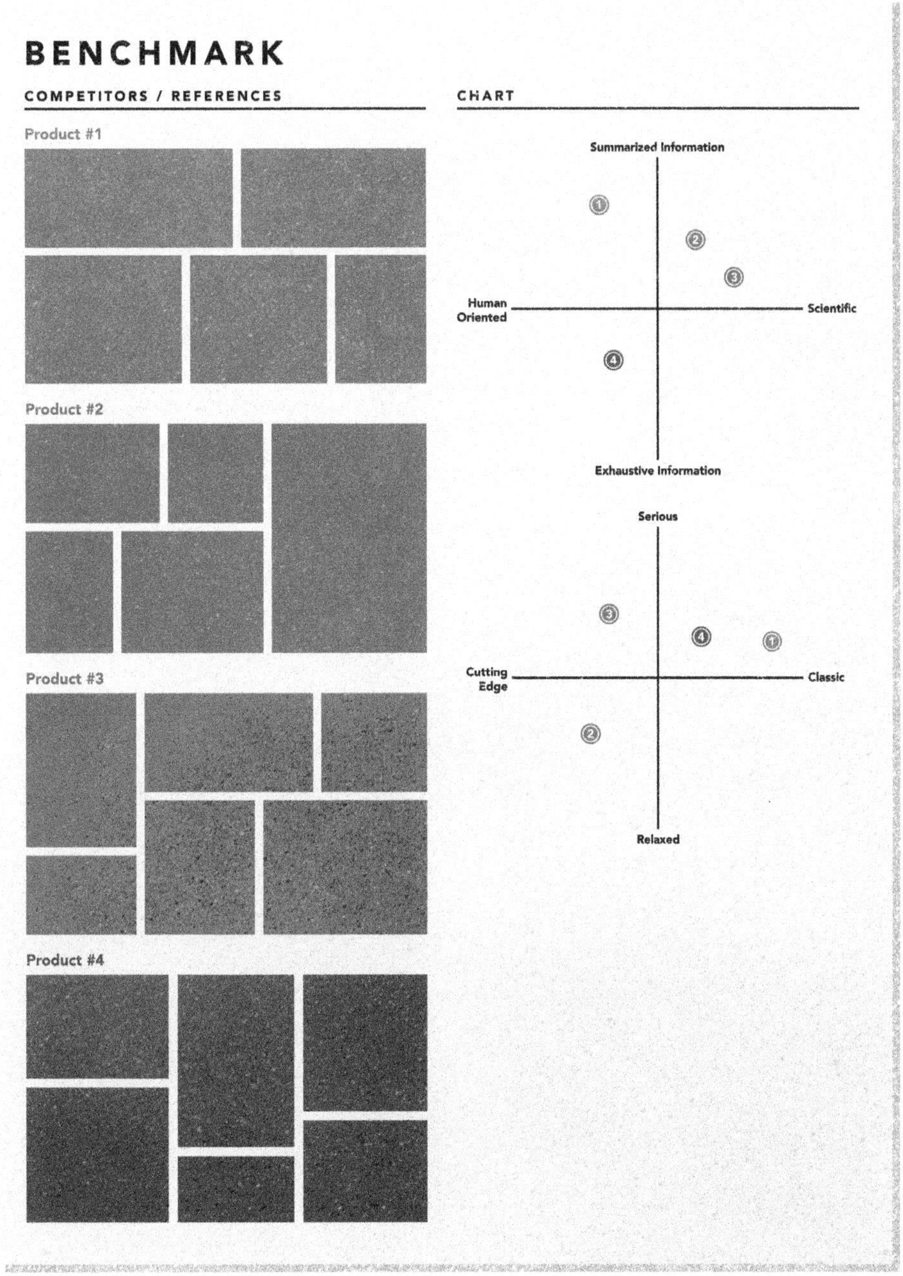

BENCHMARK

COMPETITORS / REFERENCES

CHART

Product #1

Product #2

Product #3

Product #4

Summarized Information

①
②
③

Human Oriented — Scientific

④

Exhaustive Information

Serious

③
④ ①

Cutting Edge — Classic

②

Relaxed

Figure 3/ Design Benchmark deliverable

For the Cartesian Graphic, you could pick, for instance, the dichotomies of "human-oriented / scientific" and "summarized information / exhaustive information" and position the various products in between, as it can be seen in the right side of Figure 3. There could be, for instance, a shortage regarding applications with a scientific approach that present information as a summary. That could be a space in the market where a new product could be successful, since it would be different from existing products.

References

1. The Design Matrix: A powerful tool for guiding client input (Bridget Fahrland, 2011)

CHAPTER 6

User Journey

Once you know who your Personas are and what goals they want to achieve, you have to envision how they will accomplish these goals with your product. You should think about how Personas will get to know the product and start using it, in what contexts they will use it, what tasks they will perform and how to make them repeatedly come back to the product.

Why

The consequence of starting a design process immediately with the GUI design, focusing on individual screens rather than in a flow or journey, is a poor user experience with the user feeling confused, lost or demotivated, and increasing the changes of loss of users. Neglecting the way and context in which the user goes from one screen, step, or task to another may lead to:

- Processes that demand too much investment from the user before presenting them any return;

• Lack of reassurance for the user about the actions that they have taken;

• Lack of clues telling users what they should do or where they should go next;

• Absence of proper incentives for the user to use the product again or explore more of its possibilities.

The main goal of the User Journey step is to guarantee that this does not happen. Its objective is to create a journey that is, above all else, cohesive and simple ensuring that users do not feel lost at any time and incentivating them to prolong your product usage.

What

User Journeys consist of Persona based scenarios merged with insights from two other frameworks/models:[1] the Pirate Metrics framework and [2] the Hook Model. Next we will define each in order to provide a better understanding of this step.

PERSONA-BASED SCENARIOS

Persona based-scenarios are "concise narrative descriptions of one or more Personas using a product or service to achieve a specific goal (...) using a story to describe an ideal experience from the Persona's perspective"[3]. While often confused with use cases and user stories, they are different techniques, with different focus and levels of granularity.

User stories, despite their name, are not actually stories. Instead they consist of informal phrased requirements (for instance, "As a user, I want to login into my account") and are less focused on possible scenarios as they do not describe the users' entire highlevel workflow nor what the users' end goals are. User Journeys are more akin to epics – with the proviso that epics focus on function and presentation of the interface and interactions rather than on user behaviors.

Use cases, by contrast, are based on exhaustive descriptions of the system's functional requirements of an oftentimes transactional nature and focused on low-level user action and resulting system response. A use case allows a complete cataloguing of user tasks for different classes of users but it describes little or nothing about how they should be prioritized and thus treats all possible user interactions as equally likely and important.

Software engineering rather than UX design sits at the root of these techniques, as they do not address human factors as usefulness or human perception, without which you cannot properly prioritize the various considerations and deliver an overall good user experience.

55

PIRATE METRICS

Pirate Metrics is a quantitative framework that can (and should) be used to evaluate a product's performance. Table 5 identifies the five metrics contemplated by the framework.

Pirate Metric Stages	
Acquisition	You acquire the user. For a SaaS product, this usually means a sign up.
Activation	The user uses your product, indicating a good first visit.
Retention	The user continues to use your product, indicating they like your product.
Referrals	The user likes your product so much he refers it to other new users.
Revenue	The user pays you.

Table 5/ The five metrics of the Pirate Metrics

The Hook Model is a framework that covers the elements needed to lead the user to use your product for the first time and repeat the experience on a regular basis thereafter.

Figure 4/ Visual representation of the Hook Model

56

1 - Trigger

As seen in Figure 4, the trigger is what starts the process and prompts the Persona to try your product. There are two main types of trigger: internal and external. The internal trigger is the Persona's emotions or feelings, they have their root in basic human needs. It can be a negative emotion that the user wants to stop or prevent or a positive one that they want to share but the trigger always exists regardless of whether you are offering a product. Thus the association between an internal trigger and your product is unlikely to be formed overnight and it can take weeks or months of frequent use. The internal trigger can keep users hooked in the long term, but, first, you will need to spark an initial user action and ensure that the product is used enough for repeated stimulus, that creates an association between the internal stimulus and the product. To accomplish this, you will need, first of all, external triggers that queue users with a call to action through sensory stimulation. Nir Eyal describes four types[2]:

• Paid triggers: They are the cost to get a user to use a product. Examples include advertising, search engine marketing and other marketing channels that exchange money for access. They are usually very costly and unsustainable for most business models, so while they can be used to acquire new users, other alternatives should be considered to bring existing users back.

• Earned triggers: This type of triggers are a consequence of a product getting recognition through its features or any other aspects. Some examples are favorable press mentions, hot viral videos, or featured app store placements. They can be effective, but they are also hard to replicate.

• Relationship triggers: This triggers could happen when someone tells others about a product or service, either through a like, share or word of mouth. This is a key trigger, but it has to be used carefully and in an ethical manner. When designers intentionally trick users into inviting friends or blasting a message to their social network they may see some initial growth but it will fade soon. For instance, asking users to share a Facebook page in order to receive a reward can be seen as

57

an efficient relationship trigger, but the users are not recommending the product, they are just checking a step out in order to get the reward. If it happens frequently, there can be backlash to both the product and the user.

• Owned triggers: Owned triggers are already part of the user's environment by choice. Good examples include, an app icon on the user's phone screen, an email newsletter to which users subscribe, or an app notification icon. They consistently appear and it is ultimately up to the user to opt into allowing those triggers to be shown. As long as a user agrees to receive a trigger, the company that sets it owns a share of that user's attention. While paid, earned, and relationship triggers drive new user acquisition, owned triggers focus on maintaining existing users.

58

2 - Action

Following the above flow, action is the next step and it may be defined as the behavior of the user. In the Hook Model, the term "action" does not take in consideration the difference between goals, tasks and actions, but keep in mind that, in the User Journey you should keep the focus on tasks and not the actions taken.

3 - Reward

Following the action comes the variable reward. "What distinguishes the Hook Model from a plain vanilla feedback loop is the hook's ability to create a craving. Feedback loops are all around us, but when predictable, they do not create desire. The unsurprising response of your fridge light turning on when you open the door does not drive you to keep opening it again and again. However, add some variability to the mix - suppose a different treat magically appears in your fridge every time you open it - and voilá. Variable rewards are one of the most powerful tools"[2].

4 - Investment

The last phase of the Hook Model, in the bottom-left corner of Figure 4, is the investment and it is where the user does a bit of the work. It occurs when the user provides input to the product such as time, data, effort, social capital, or money. It implies a task that improves the service the next go-around, such as inviting friends, stating preferences, building visual assets, etc...

It is important to emphasize that the investment only comes after the variable reward and it is a common mistake to present actions that demand investment from the users before giving them a reward. For instance, having too many preferences to set up or a number of steps before concluding a signup reduces the chances of the user moving on to the next phase and increases the probability of losing users in the process.

Following the three frameworks described here – Persona-based scenarios, Pirate Metrics and the Hook Model – you will be able to get a much better understanding of a Persona's expected behavior and be sure you do not forget any stage of the user interaction with your product. In the next section we will explore with greater depth exactly how to bring them together in an actual User Journey.

59

Until now, we have seen that the User Journey step consists on a Persona based scenario combined with insights from Pirate Metrics and the Hook Model and we have defined each of those concepts. In this section, we will make it clear exactly how the metrics and the triggers should be approached with reference to the product's users.

The User Journey starts with the five metrics identified in the Pirate Metrics model: acquisition, activation, retention, referral and revenue. With each of these metrics you should include a consideration for the user's mood and emotions each time you expect it to change. Typically, each stage, and the overall User Journey, should follow a pattern where there is a crescendo in the emotion's positivity: either the user starts with negative emotions and ends with positive ones or the user starts with positive emotions and ends with positive emotions of greater intensity. Taking a measure of the user's mood at each point of the journey will help you to make decisions about the visual interface later in the Mood Board and GUI steps and will also help you contemplate details like confirmation messages and other feedback elements that are crucial for a good user experience. Since each stage is slightly different, we will present them in detail, using the triggers from the Hook Model that was introduced earlier.

In the first stage of the Pirate Metrics model, acquisition, you should start by explaining the context where you expect the Persona to use your product for the first time. Here you should identify the trigger that will prompt the user to find the product and present the Persona's end-goal that was defined in the User Research step. Then, you should describe the first task that the Persona needs to carry out in order to become a user (it can be a signup or downloading the app, for instance) and, ideally, present the reward that the user will receive once the task is completed. The activation stage is where the Persona actually starts using your product and it occurs after the first phase (from the user's point of view there is no interruption between both phases). The following stage is the user investment, which consists in the different tasks that the user should perform in order to become engaged with the product. These tasks should lead to the achievement of the user's end-goal and this stage is finished when the user leaves the app after the first usage. Do not forget about the transitions between each task; everything has to be fluid and you should describe all of the involved steps. This ensures that you will end with a fluid user experience in which the user always knows what to do next and is encouraged to stay and prolong their use of your product. Also, it will ensure its efficiency, avoiding unnecessary steps that make the process longer and thus reduce the chances of the user actually completing it.

61

The retention stage should describe a later usage of the product in a different moment. You explain the context in which the user exists at this time and the trigger (both the context and the trigger may be different from the ones from the first usage). Next, you explain how the user will come back to the product and describe the reward that they will have once they return. Finally, you describe the investment task that the user will execute this time and which may demand a deeper level of product use than the one presented in the activation metric. The referral stage may or may not follow the retention stage. More specifically, it may happen in the current stage or during future product usage. If the referral is supposed to happen at a later time, you should describe the new context; if the referral can happen in the current stage of use, you should identify the trigger that will make the user want to share your product, the task that will allow it, and the reward that will be received for sharing. The revenue stage may actually be presented before or after the referral (or even before the retention). This is where you explain how your product will be profitable. Possible models could include user generated revenue (for instance, the user paying for your product) or through other strategies like advertising. If the revenue model demands user investment you should describe the trigger that will cause them to invest. In both scenarios - user investment or advertisement - you should include the reward that the user gets from the investment, which could include the users achieving some of their goals or being granted access to information and/or products in which they are interested via the advertisement.

In the end, you will have the outline of a journey that the ideal user will undertake from the moment they get to know your product until they achieve their desired goals through it. To conclude this step, we will provide a practical example in the next section.

Examples

Imagine that your product is an app to book flights and hotels and your Personas are tourists travelling solo who want to plan their holiday (end goal) and are worried about staying safe abroad while traveling alone.

You start the User Journey in the acquisition stage. The context where your Persona gets to know your product could be while they are at home at night watching YouTube videos from travel vloggers on a tablet. The trigger could be a sponsored video from a famous youtuber where your product is recommended. The first action that the Persona would take in order to become a user is to press the link presented in the video description that will take them to the app download page at the store. They will then download the app and could possibly sign up with a Facebook account. Here, you should think carefully on how the signup and user validation will work. Maybe the user will have to exit the app and go to their email to provide confirmation and then return to the app (this process should always be described in the User Journey). Once the user is logged in to your app the reward can consist of several travel destination ideas which fires their imagination and gets them excited (user moods).

At that point, your Persona will be considered an actual user, so you move to the activation stage. During the activation, in this case, the tasks performed by the user may include things like browsing different destination ideas, searching for a particular travel route, or budgeting for specific dates. During those tasks the user may go through several moods, from excited about a new, distant, and remote destination to worried about the security of travelling to that place or the reliability of hotels. Therefore, you should lay out some strategies to deal with the users' emotions and conduct them to the desired emotional state. This could mean displaying reviews from other users or detailing the certification process for hotels, for example. Then, in terms of the user investment, you could present tasks like filling in a profile with their preferences and save travel plans or hotels for later.

This investment in the activation component will be closely linked to the trigger of the retention part. For instance, the user preferences may be used to build a customized newsletter that would be sent to them with some regularity. The specific way in which this would work is what you should describe in the retention.

Regarding the revenue, you could grant access to discounts and

63

special offers to users who subscribe to your product. For the purpose of referral you could offer a voucher to the users who had referred your product to others and that would also work as a trigger.

These examples are presented to flesh out the concepts involved in the User Journey. A real User Journey has a story telling perspective and should contemplate all of the main features of your app, since this document will be the source from which you will obtain the product features to put together the Decision Matrix, the next step of the process.

References

1. Pirate Metrics: Actionable Analytics for Your Business (2012-2014)

2. Hooked: How to Build Habit-Forming Products (Nir Eyal and Ryan Hoover, 2014)

3. About face 3: The essentials of interaction design (Alan Cooper, Robert Reimann and David Cronin, 2007)

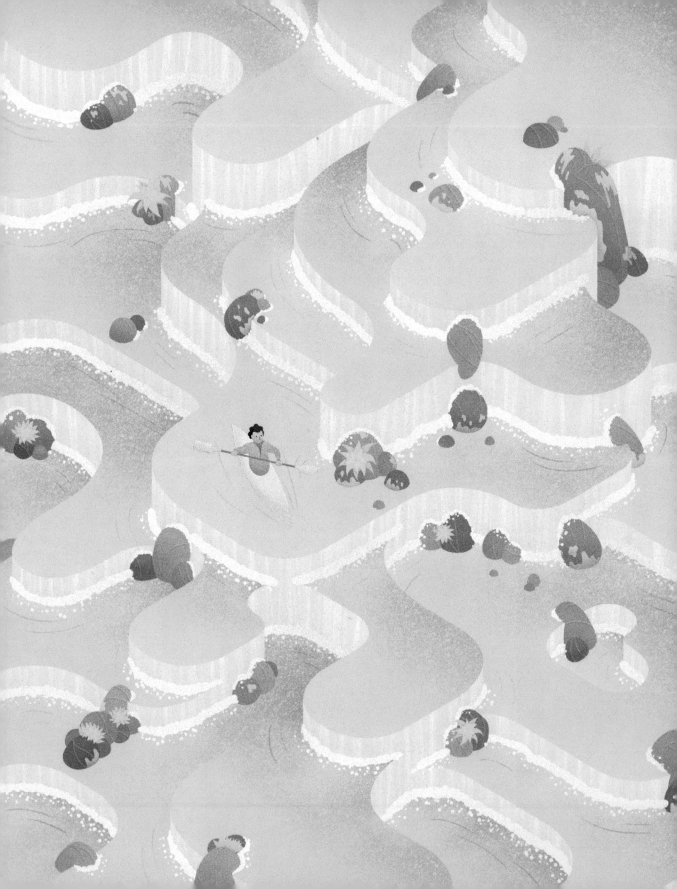

CHAPTER 7

Decision Matrix

If you were to visualize a good design process, it would appear in the shape of a diamond, as depicted in Figure 5. In the early steps, you generate ideas to explore various possibilities and then you start narrowing these down by picking certain paths over others, as the arrows show through a diverge and converge process on the left-hand side. The last step – the User Journey - is the peak of the Ideation phase, generating numerous new ideas about possible features to create an idealized User Journey. Now, at the Decision Matrix step, highlighted in Figure 5 by the dark triangle, you have reached the break point, when you start narrowing down and choosing your approach. This is the project step where the product team will stop thinking about new features and start choosing from all of the available ideas.

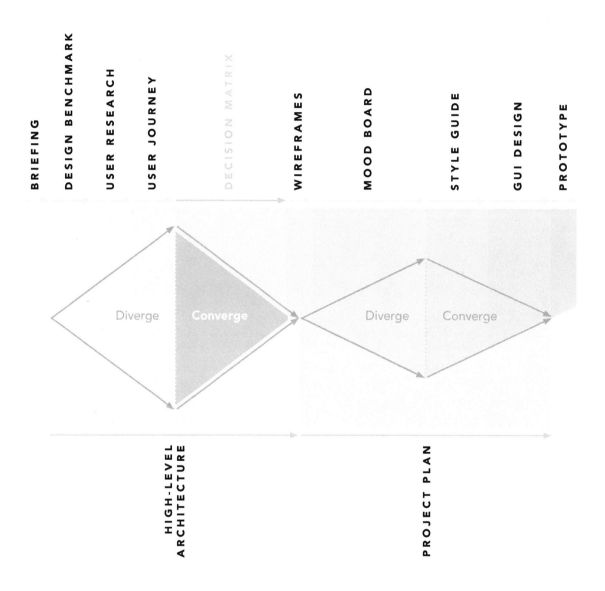

BRIEFING

DESIGN BENCHMARK

USER RESEARCH

USER JOURNEY

DECISION MATRIX

WIREFRAMES

MOOD BOARD

STYLE GUIDE

GUI DESIGN

PROTOTYPE

Diverge

Converge

Diverge

Converge

HIGH-LEVEL ARCHITECTURE

PROJECT PLAN

Figure 5/ Diamond-shaped representation of PDP

Why

The design must be carefully thought out to avoid building castles in the sky and prevent what we call the "feature creep black hole", which is when features that are not relevant to the current product stage continue to be added. The reality is that the budget and time limitations will probably not allow for implemention of all of the proposed ideas. Features need to be prioritized so that the team is able to build a working product that can be released and tested as soon as possible, while also addressing the users' needs[1]. This is what is commonly know in the software development industry as a Minimum Viable Product (MVP), an expression coined by Frank Robinson in 2001 that was popularized by many others in the following years. There are two reasons for using this approach: firstly, because some opportunities may have a small time window in the market and, secondly, because one should manage the risks associated with new products and ideas.

The bottom line is that you need to prioritize all of the features that you would like to have in the product, deciding which ones are fundamental to a first version and which can be left until a later stage without compromising the basic usability dimension. Prioritizing features at this point, before the design is complete, allows you to save time and end up with a higher quality MVP. Not only you will not spend time designing features that you will not implement, but also your MVP will be designed to work with and without certain features, ensuring that no screen or navigation path is broken if you do not implement low-priority features. Those features that were omitted can quickly be added later through small adjustments.

What

The Decision Matrix consists of a list of all features, extracted from the User Journey, organized in epics and user stories, and rated according to the user and business goals.

How

As it was previously mentioned, this is a sensitive phase because most product managers struggle with the idea of giving up certain features without realizing that these might not be relevant for the current stage of the product's lifecycle. After doing market research, undertaking the User Research step, and after much time spent maturing the product vision, many ideas will have been generated and no one likes to discard ideas that can improve the product. However, it is all a matter of mindset. You are not giving up features, just prioritizing and leaving some to a later phase after the product launch. The release does not mean the end of product development or of design thinking. It is just one more step in this cycle, one in which you will make the product public and get real user feedback, so you can have insights for a new round of Ideation, Execution, building, testing, launch and feedback. No feature that you decided not to include in the next release will have been discarded - only postponed. You need to be methodical about the way you choose features and assure the product owner that the product will not stop improving after launch. Next, we will show you how to carry out this process.

1. List epics - play with the levels of complexity for each user story

First of all, you need to list all of the epics that you want to implement, which can be done by organizing one epic per line in a spreadsheet. Then, for each, write down the different user stories.

Start by conceptualizing the simplest user story possible. Then, write increasingly technically demanding user stories. This will allow you to easily allocate the different user stories to different project phases without compromising the high-level epic. With this user stories list in mind, we will move on to how to rate the user stories and epics.

2. Rate according to user goals

In the User Research step, you collected and compiled the information about the user goals, the core of Personas. In the Decision Matrix, you will return to those goals in order to start the first diverge process of PDP, prioritizing the user stories you have considered so far. To do this, use a scoring system like the one depicted in Table 6 to define a user story's importance to accomplish each user goal from each persona.

72

Score 3	The goal cannot be accomplished without the feature. It means that the feature is essential for the product.
Score 2	The goal can be achieved without it but the feature would compromise the user experience. It means that the product may work without it but this would have an impact on the product's quality.
Score 1	The goal can be achieved without the feature. The feature's absence does not impact the product's quality or end goals.

Table 6/ Scoring system for the Decision Matrix

Afterwards, give different weights to each Persona according to their priority (established at the User Research step). Then use the following formula to calculate each user story's final score:

$$\frac{(persona1Goal1Value + persona1Goal2Valuen + persona1Goal3Value) \times 3 + (persona2Goal1Value + persona2Goal2Value + persona2Goal3Value) \times 2 + (persona3Goal1Value + persona3Goal2Value + persona3Goal3Value) \times 1}{3+2+1} = FeatureUserRate$$

Table 7/ Formula to calculate feature's final score according to the user goals

73

Once the scoring is done for the user goals, you will do something similar from the vantage point of the business. Here you will use the Pirate Metrics framework (presented in the previous chapter – acquisition, activation, retention, revenue and referral) to rate how important each user story is to accomplish them, taking into consideration the stage of the product's development. If you are launching a new product, acquisition and activation will be of utmost importance. If you are in a second version and you already have a few users, you may want to focus on retention and referral. Depending on the urgency that you have in getting revenue you may want to attribute a higher weight to these last two stages or a lower one in the case in which you have to to leave them for a later stage, when your users are more open to paying for use of the product. Here is an example:

$$\frac{\begin{array}{l} \text{AcquisitionRate} \quad \textbf{x3} \quad + \\ \text{ActivationRate} \quad \textbf{x3} \quad + \\ \text{RetentionRate} \quad \textbf{x1} \quad + \\ \text{ReferalRate} \quad \textbf{x1} \quad + \\ \text{RevenueRate} \quad \textbf{x1} \end{array}}{3+3+1+1+1} = \text{FeatureBusinessRate}$$

Table 8/ Formula to calculate feature's final score according to the business goals

4. Check product usefulness VS business model

Up to this point, you have scored two values for each user story: one reflecting their usefulness and another reflecting the business model needs. This double scoring system is essential to make sure that the product meets both the user goals and the business goals, which are certainly different from the start. You need to check if these two scores are aligned before moving on to the next section. If you have several user stories in which there is a substantial divergence between the values for the user goals and business categories, you should check if the business model's sustainability is at risk. This can happen if, for instance, user stories that have a score of 3 on the user goals also have a score of 1 on the business model revenue rate and you are highly dependent on the generated revenue. Lastly, make a simple average of both scores and you will end up with each user stories' priority level.

75

5. Reducing your target audience (if needed)

After prioritization, if you end up with a number of user stories with high priority (a score of 3) that exceeds the time and budget that you have available for the first implementation you need to rethink this step.

In the User Research step, we stated that you should not list all Personas goals, but only keep those which are essential. This will enable you to avoid a situation in which you have an extensive list of goals that you cannot address properly. With this is mind, review your ratings and ensure that user stories that you have rated with a score of 3 are actually important to their respective goals, without forcing the ratings to fit your project plan. Then, start by reducing the number of goals that you are trying to address by reducing your scope to the main persona's goals (according to the persona's priotization done in the User Research step). Remove the columns for additional Personas and check all the formulas to account for the change then recalculate each user story rating afterwards.

If you still end up with too many user stories scored as 3, choose only one of the main persona's goals and stick with it. Your app may do only one thing, but if it does it well, people will use it. In this case, remove the collumns of the main persona goals you discarded and calculate the score again. Lastly, check that the most important user stories in terms of business goals were not removed to ensure that the business model is still viable. After this process is complete, you will have the leanest product that is still viable and implementable.

Examples

Imagine that you are designing a product that allows users to save and consult documentation and the user end goal is to easily find the necessary or desired documentation. You will probably want an epic that consists of a display table with all of the user's documents. This can be conceptualized with different levels of complexity, as seen in Table 9, in which a set of different possible user stories are listed showing documents in a table view format

Epic #1 (E1)
This user sees a documents index table showing document.

User Story 1	This user sees a documents index table showing document name, type, status, author, creation date and last saving date.
User Story 2	This user can sort documents by date or status.
User Story 3	This user can filter documents by type, author and subject.
User Story 4	The user can adjust manually each collumn width through drag and drop.

Table 9/ Different user stories for a single epic

Other epics can be valuable, like scanning documents directly into the documents repository, which can also have several degrees of complexity. Further versions could explore additional possibilities for scanning documents, as seen below in Table 10.

Epic #2 (E2)
Scan documents directly into the documents repository.

User Story 1	The user takes a photo and adds it as an image to the documents repository.
User Story 2	The user can choose to aggregate several images and save them as one single document in the repository.
User Story 3	The user can convert the photo to a text pdf.

Table 10/ Different user stories for an additional epic

78

Imagine that to implement both epics in their most complete form (all of their user stories) you would have to go over the time or budget constraints of the project. You can either choose to implement only one of the epics in its first and most complete version or implement both in their most basic versions. By analyzing the epics' relevance to the user's end goals you may come to the conclusion that the first epic has a higher priority. You will always need a way to present documents so that they are easily accessible and your app would work even if it just answered that singular goal. However, if you add an epic to scan documents but you are not offering an easy way to present them, you are not answering the user goal at all.

The data acquired in the User Research is essential to choose and define the best approach here. Does the user frequently deal with long file names that can be problematic for the small screen size of the device for which you are designing? Is the amount of paperwork more important? Even if, overall, Epic 1 (E1) is more important than Epic 2 (E2), user stories 1 and 2 of E2 may be more important than the user story 4 of E1. After rating each line according to the user goals you may end with the following priority:

E1 v1 ⟩ E1 v2 ⟩ E1 v3 ⟩ E2 v1 ⟩ E2 v2 ⟩ E2 v3 ⟩ E2 v4 ⟩ E1 v4

Table 11/ Possible user story priority for the previous example

As you move on to the Technical Assessment and Project Plan steps, you may have to make minor adjustments. For instance, when facing more precise estimates you may see that the budget or time frames available after implementing E2 v3 is enough to implement E1 v4 but

80

	USER STORY		FEATURE	PERSONA #1	
				USER GOAL #1	USER GOAL #2
				Get all their admin paperwork digitalized and centralised.	Know the financial status of the company balance at any time.
1	Registering in the platform	1.1	Add a user in the backoffice after an offline on boarding.	1	1
		1.2	Requests an account in the front-office by inserting all the information and documentation necessary for validation and approve or reject account requests in the back-office.	1	1
2	Show documents in a table view format	2.1	Documents index table showing document name, type, status, author, creation date and last saving date.	3	1
		2.2	Sort documents by date or status.	2	1
		2.3	Filter documents by type, author and subject.	2	1
		2.4	Choose the columns showing the date.	2	1
3	Insert banking transfers in the platform	3.1	Input the transfer information manually into the platform.	1	3
		3.2	Import bank movements from CSV files.	3	3
		3.3	Copy, from the bank website, the text relative to the movements and past the text in the platform, having the system automatically parsing and placing the text in the right fields.	3	3

Figure 6/ Decision Matrix deliverable with user and business goals rated by their relevance not E2 v4. Aside from these small adjustments in the rating of low priority items, you will have at the end of this step the foundations for the Project Plan, based on user goals rather than just a pure engineering perspective, observable in the following figure.

USER GOALS AVERAGE	BUSINESS GOALS					BUSINESS GOALS AVERAGE	TOTAL SCORE
	acquisition	activation	retention	growth	revenue		
1	3	1	2	1	1	2,4	1,7
1	2	1	1	2	1	2	1,5
2	1	1	3	1	1	1,8	1,9
1,5	1	1	2	1	1	1,6	1,55
1,5	1	1	2	1	1	1,6	1,55
1,5	1	1	2	1	1	1,6	1,55
2	1	3	1	1	1	2,2	2,1
3	1	2	2	1	1	2	2,5
3	1	2	2	1	1	2	2,5

References

1. Using prioritization matrices to inform UX decisions (Sarah Gibbons, 2018)

CHAPTER 8

Wireframes

The Wireframes are the first step of the Execution phase. This is when the requirements materialize into something visual for the first time. In many cases, the desire to save time tempts the designers or the product manager to disregard this step. However, as we will see next, the extra time needed for the Wireframes is worth it because this step increases quality and reduces the project's required investment of time and effort.

Why

Changes made in the final design always take more time and effort than those made during any of the preceding steps in the process. However, inevitably, in the first few contacts that the product owner has with the interface, change requests will come up. From changes in the layout structure to changes in the content/copy, or even in the requirements.

Making these changes in the final design is an incredibly time consuming task, since for each change it is necessary to take into account the style or, more specifically, colors, fonts, margins and alignments in each instance and on each screen. In the absence of the adequate time and a keen eye for detail, reworking features during the final design stage is one of the main causes for inconsistent interfaces, and/or a sloppy final deliveries. The Wireframes are a quick way to experiment and show different options to the product owner, helping you to validate all the mentioned aspects of the product. Thus, this step helps you achieving higher quality products and deliverables by reducing structural changes in the final designs. Additionally, by jumping directly to the screens with the final stylized design, the product owner (and whoever is responsible for the design) is forced to approve several aspects of the design work at the same time. Since the visual details of a product are more noticeable, there is the tendency to work on these, without paying much attention to deeper UX problems. Wireframes help correct this tendency.

This step allows you to focus on questions such as navigation, architecture, content and information hierarchy. Besides that, Wireframes make it easier to find structural solutions to design challenges that would, otherwise, demand too much visual styling. This becomes abundantly clear during the hierarchical ordering of elements and content. A good information architecture - achieved with efficient content division throughout the various pages or sections of the interface and with the strategic positioning of certain elements in the page – can make the elements and content hierarchy clear even in situations where visual styling is absent. When this work is not done and the hierarchy is communicated only through the stylized design, the end result is usually the excessive styling of elements and the multiplication of numerous visual styles. This causes confusion for the user and creates additional work for the front-end developers that are forced to multiply CSS classes in what, most of the times, ends up being a case-by-case approach.

What

The Wireframes may be defined as the screens' skeleton. They are the layout without styling and are only a high-level black and white sketch.

How

The Wireframes should cover all of the main screens and in order to meet the provided expectations it is necessary that they also show some level of detail. The level of detail from Wireframes varies according to the industry, since they are dependent on the objectives for which they are being used and of the phase of the project in which they are carried out. Frequently, they are only sketches with the goal of registering and articulating ideas, an approach that is valuable at the start of the creative process, when there is a lot of uncertainty about the final design. However, to achieve the advantages discussed in the previous sub-section, it is important to make them in a way that certain points may be clarified at this step. Make sure to detail the following aspects:

- Navigation and sub navigation;
- Textual and multimedia content in the final sections;
- The complete list of forms and fields;
- The final layout (final positioning of various content sections).

With this approach to Wireframes, the visual designer will not have

85

to change the element's places in the next step and hence will only need to define aspects such as specific margins, font sizes, positioning of small elements such as actions ("see more", for instance) or details such as the publication date of an article. This guarantees that there is no redundancy in the work done, allowing the deliverable of this step to be the foundations of the final design. With this approach, the visual designer can dedicate more of their effort to the creation of a visual atmosphere that produces the desired experience:

Examples

In Figure 7 you can see an example of a deliverable that could be generated from this step, showing the skeleton of a website without any of the styling that will be added in the following steps of PDP.

Further Reading

A project guide to UX design: For user experience designers in the field or in the making (Russ Unger and Carolyn Chandler, 2009)

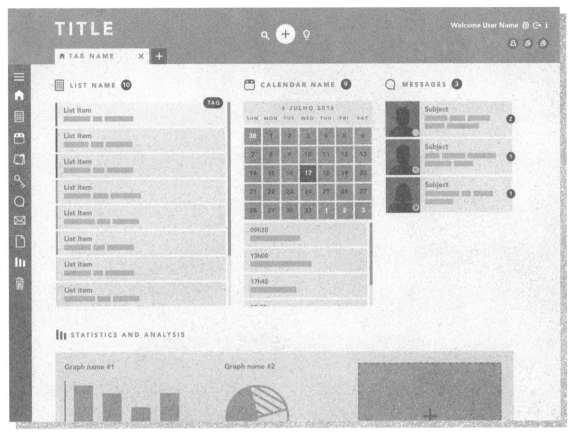

Figure 7/ Wireframes deliverable example

CHAPTER 9

Mood Board

When it comes to creating the look & feel of a product, the possibilities are endless. This step is the last in the Ideation phase and aims to explore and reach a decision about the different style options. This is the moment in which the visual designer takes the main role on PDP.

Why

To guide styling choices you have, by now, an indication of the user experience goals, from the User Research step, and the positioning of the product, decided in the Design Benchmark step, as well as some notes regarding the product owner's preferences. However, both the experience goals and positioning appear as abstract concepts consisting of, for instance, something that transmits the idea of "trustable" or "modern". These concepts might correspond to different visual approaches in the mind of the designer and in the mind of the product owner. If you jump directly to production, without first clarifying the way in which concepts materialize, you risk wasting time in the Execution of final screens that do not meet the product owner's expectations regarding visual style.

The Mood Board allows you to test more rapidly different visual approaches, while at the same time observing the reaction of the product owner and lining up concepts. If this experimentation was carried out directly with the interface, producing different interfaces with distinct styling would be more time consuming due to the time that it takes to apply styles. Besides that, producing a number of distinctively styled interfaces to get feedback from the product owner is not the best approach because it requires adopting very specific stylistic choices, making it difficult to understand if an eventual change requested by the product owner is due to disagreement with the approach in itself or to a more minor objection to a specific style applied. Even the product owner may not be able to identify the precise source of disagreement when confronted with a complete design that scatters the team's attention across various elements. This is a scenario that usually ends in multiple iterative development cycles in which approval is denied because the changes made do not address the origins of any given objection.

Additionally, if the product owner is developing not only the product but also the brand, the Mood Board may be used as a guide or support material by the marketing team. However, the value of the Mood Board in itself is minimal for the product owner. Its added value is in making it easier for the visual designer to communicate abstract concepts to the product owner, allowing the former to experiment quickly with different visual approaches and use observations about the product owner's reaction to make decisions about the final design.

What

The Mood Board consists of a canvas that gathers various inspirational materials, communicating the values and emotions that the product should transmit.

How

The first step in the construction of a Mood Board is the analysis of experience goals (User Research) and positioning (Design Benchmark) in order to understand which emotions and state of mind the product should impart to the user. You should then build out two Mood Boards, both presenting the same set of values and emotions but with approaches as visually dissimilar as possible in order to clarify concepts and obtain an aesthetic direction. It is also important that the materials used for the Mood Board draw upon the most diverse pool of source materials possible, going beyond the industry and even the medium in question when practicable. The designer should look to references such as magazines, books, CD covers, and more. This is one of the keys for innovation and by including examples that are not based on other digital interfaces it is easier to direct the discussion to the desired mood and avoid focusing on specific GUI styles.

When the Mood Boards are done, you should meet with the product owner in order to obtain feedback about the path to be taken. To guarantee that choices are being made with conviction, special attention should be paid to the product owner's reactions when facing the different options presented. Sometimes the product owner, due to a lack of palpable material to elaborate an opinion, may not have definite views on a particular design element and will prefer to wait until the Mood Board is applied to the product interface.

91

However, changing the visual direction in the GUI step is more time consuming and should be avoided if possible. So, you must be observant regarding communication between the product owner and the visual designer and not be afraid to explore more visual options until both stakeholders are comfortable with the path taken. The designer is the team member with the most experience in this area and should advise the other members of the team about when it is best to explore more examples.

Examples

Imagine that the experience goals that you have are adventure, exploring, discover, fun, and immersion and the positioning of the product is in the informative and big-picture quadrant. The concepts "informative" and "fun" may send you to oranges and yellows and the "immersion" and "big-picture" concepts may guide you to landscapes and full-page images. The "exploring" and "discover" concepts may be approached through dreams and scientific discovery going beyond the limits of what is known or through exploring scenery and nature in a more down-to-earth sense. In Figure 8 you can see two Mood Boards that could result from these concepts with different approaches to the same product.

MOOD BOARD #2

Figure 8/ Two examples of Mood Boards for the same product

MOOD BOARD #1

ZEMBOOK TYPE

One morning, when Gregor Samsa woke from troubled dreams, he found himself transformed in his bed into a horrible vermin. He lay on his armour-like back, and if he lifted his head a little he could see his brown belly, slightly domed and divided by arches into stiff sections. The bed was hardly able to cover it and seemed

Woven silk pyjamas exchanged for blue quartz.

A wonderful serenity has taken possession of my entire soul, like these sweet mornings of spring which I enjoy with my whole heart. I am alone, and feel the charm

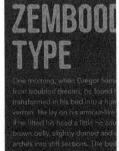

QUICK
ZEPHYRS
BLOW,
VEXING
DAFT JIM.

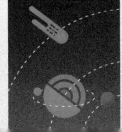

CHAPTER 10

Style Guide

Once the Ideation phase is completed, the Style Guide appears as the first step in the Execution phase, when the direction chosen up to this point turns into specific artistic choices and when the interface starts to take shape. Given the practical nature of the Execution phase, the presentation and theoretical explanation of the embedded process in the next couple of steps is going to be shorter. However, it does not mean they are less critical or demanding than the others.

Why

One of the most important aspects of a good user experience is the interface's consistency throughout its various sections, pages, and interaction points. The graphic style of each element provides fundamental indicators to the user, pointing to their current location in the application flow's context, directing the attention to the most relevant information and showing clickable elements, for instance. The usage of consistent style patterns throughout the product allows the user to perceive the information quicker and with a smaller margin for error. This results in an easier, faster, more fluid, and reassuring user experience. Additionally, the element's styling consistency saves time and effort during implementation by simplifying the CSS.

What

The Style Guide is a document that compiles various stylized GUI elements (buttons, headers, text blocks, images, etc.), and functions as a style library that will be used in the GUI Design step.

How

The next sub-sections will take you through the process of creating a Style Guide. However, one of the most important things to build a good Style Guide is to examine a wide variety of visual references materials and understand how they communicate emotions and concepts with visual elements. Knowledge of the Color Theory, Gestalt Principles, and composition rules are also very important for this step.

1. Define the color pallet

Go back to the Mood Board elaborated in the last step, extract the colors from it, and adjust them in terms of contrast, saturation and brightness. The objective of this exercise is to create a harmonious combination that guarantees the application's visibility and legibility in its typical context. The number of colors used may vary, but, as guidance, it is useful to think about the following:

• Background color;

• Text color;

• Actions color;

• Highlights color.

In most cases, these elements will define the number of colors that you will be using in the Style Guide, but this is not a rule that is carved in stone.

97

2. Style some elements from the Wireframes

Next, you should extract some elements from the Wireframes and style them, using the defined color pallet and the visual language of the Mood Board. Some crucial elements that should be included in the Style Guide are:

• Paragraph style, titles, and other recurring textual elements (subtitles and tags, for instance);

• Buttons (preferably in their variations: inactive, active, over and pressed etc);

• Input fields (textboxes, select boxes, and other recurring input elements, also in every variation possible);

• Relevant iconography;

• Other elements that have an important role in the product

and/or are repeated throughout the Wireframes (e.g. graphics, tables, widgets, etc.)

The objective is not to create an exhaustive list of all graphic elements used in the interface, but rather only those which have a more frequent or relevant presence and, for that reason, determine the look and feel of the application.

3. Highlight other important graphic elements

Among the stylized aspects that make the leap from the Mood Board, we should also highlight:

• The dimensions of margins (if there is more or less negative space);

• The contrast and delimitation between elements (if each element is individualized through their color, line or negative space and how it stands out from the background);

• The angles used - both in the font and in objects such as containers and input fields – and whether they are straight or rounded up).

Usually, changes to the colors pallet come up during the styling of these elements. Similarly, during the GUI Design, the next stage, some changes to the Style Guide are also common. Good examples are related to the color contrast, the eventual gray scales or the text style, however, no relevant change should be made from this step forward.

4. Create two Style Guides for each Mood Board

Similar to what happened in the last step, here you should also create at least two Style Guides, both based on the same Mood Board. These should explore slightly different stylistic options in order to present distinctive possibilities to the product owner and allow the choice between different color pallets and fonts, but always in the same mood. If the product owner does not feel satisfied with any of the options, you should provide elaborated alternatives until you reach a consensus. Some product owners may have difficulty in picking a visual style before seeing it applied to the interface and in those cases it is useful to stylize a few screens according to the Style Guide to get higher quality feedback. However, you should not stylize many screens before the product owner's approval is received.

Spend as much time as needed in the Style Guide, experimenting until the product owner feels completely satisfied with a given option. Going forward with an option that does not generate much enthusiasm will consequently mean more time wasted during the GUI step.

99

Examples

In Figure 9 you can observe two examples of Style Guides based on one of the Mood Boards presented in the last step. These are two options that come from the same mood, reflecting the stylistic choices made on the Style Guide.

STYLE GUIDE

COLORS

#FFA726	#EF6C00	#E53935	#FFDEB6	#1E0D00

TEXT STYLES

Headers

SECTIONS, TAGS
& BUTTONS

Content

Small Text

font: Font Name
font-weight: Bold

font: Font Name
font-weight: Bold
text-transform: Uppercase
character-spacing: 3

font: Font Name
font-weight: Book

font: Font Name
font-weight: Book

GRAPHIC ELEMENTS

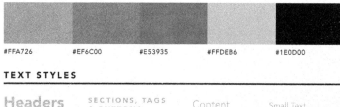

Text Header

SUBTITLE GOES HERE

Lorem ipsum dolor sit amet, consectetur adipiscing elit. Nunc consectetur at sapien eget congue. Aliquam quis rhoncus eros. Pellentesque molestie sagittis massa, eget porta lorem efficitur sit amet. Orci varius natoque penatibus et magnis dis parturient montes, nascetur ridiculus mus. Etiam efficitur tellus ac est bibendum, in aliquet nunc vulputate. Curabitur tincidunt a metus sit amet efficitur. Ut porta molestie nisl vitae consectetur.

Graph Header

SUBTITLE GOES HERE

Jan 2017   Feb 2017   Mar 2017   Apr 2017

FORMS

Form Header

FIELD TITLE

FIELD TITLE

Field Content Active

FIELD TITLE

Field Content Done

FIELD TITLE

Choose

FIELD TITLE

Option 1
Option 2
Option 3
Option 4

MAIN BUTTON

SECONDARY BUTTON

UNACTIVE BUTTON

STYLE GUIDE

COLORS

#FF8A65	#8D6E63	#FFA726	#FFE082	#1E0D00

TEXT STYLES

HEADERS

font: Font Name
font-weight: Bold
text-transform: Uppercase
character-spacing: 3

Sections, Tags & Buttons

font: Font Name
font-weight: Bold

Content

font: Font Name
font-weight: Book

Small Text

font: Font Name
font-weight: Book

GRAPHIC ELEMENTS

TEXT HEADER

Subtitle goes here

Lorem ipsum dolor sit amet, consectetur adipiscing elit. Nunc consectetur at sapien eget congue. Aliquam quis rhoncus eros. Pellentesque molestie sagittis massa, eget porta lorem efficitur sit amet. Orci varius natoque penatibus et magnis dis parturient montes, nascetur ridiculus mus. Etiam efficitur tellus ac est bibendum, in aliquet nunc vulputate. Curabitur tincidunt a metus sit amet efficitur. Ut porta molestie nisl vitae consectetur.

GRAPH HEADER

Subtitle goes here

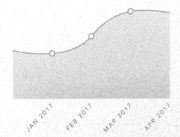

JAN 2017   FEB 2017   MAR 2017   APR 2017

FORMS

FORM HEADER

Field Title

Field Title

Field Content Active

Field Title

Field Content Done

Field Title

Choose ⌄

Field Title

Option 1   ⌃
Option 2
Option 3
Option 4

main button

secondary button

unactive button

Figure 9/ Two Style Guides for the same Mood Board

CHAPTER 11

Graphic User Interface Design

The GUI Design step is what most people imagine when thinking about design. This is where the product's pages are created with their "final" appearance or, in other words, the appearance that the user will see. In the absence of a design thinking process, most projects usually start with this step. However, the work carried out during the preceding steps of PDP make this step much quicker. If we compare the duration of PDP with the time that is usually spent on the design of a GUI without a process (i.e. without executing the previous steps), we realize that the former usually takes considerably less time than the latter. Even when it does not, the additional time invested in PDP is reflected in a better quality product. To develop an already stylized interface, that will suffer from structural or visual changes afterward, makes it necessary to repeat all of the meticulous and time consuming interface styling. Besides that, it is also much harder to identify the problems of an interface after it is finished. Since there are already a series of variables at play, it is common to identify a superficial problem as the cause, when the real issue is actually quite fundamental. For instance, you may think that the problem is the colors used. Perhaps you think that these do not sufficiently highlight a fundamental page of the website, but the underlying issue could actually be the organization of sections in the screen (something that would be easily identified and solved in the Wireframes step).

Why

The objective of this step is to present the final screens to the product owner in order to validate the GUI Design before proceeding to the development phase. This allows you to reduce the chances of getting change requests during the implementation, something that will reduce the time available for the project's development since changes usually take less time to execute on design deliveries than on code. Besides that, this step helps front-end developers interpret the interface, guiding them through that process.

What

The deliveries in this step consist of various editable vector files and one or more PDF files with an export of the editable files that contain the main pages as they would appear in the final product.

How

The GUI results from combining the Wireframes with the Style Guide. Some small changes might be needed but, fundamentally, the layout defined before should be maintained. Since there are potentially many ways to apply the Guidelines to the layout, we recommend you avoid the application of the styling to all of the Wireframes at once. Instead, do some experimentation by using two or three different approaches to apply styling to a few selected pages (typically, the homepage and another page with more content) and obtain feedback from the product owner. After getting approval, proceed and apply the same styling to all relevant screens. The styling does not need to be applied to all screens since, usually, there are various cases in which it is possible to infer the appearance of the remaining screens based on the ones you have already styled. This method allows the style to be applied directly and automatically during the implementation phase, with the assistance of the visual designer.

Examples

In Figure 10 you can see an example of a screen stylized according to one of the Style Guides presented in the last step.

106

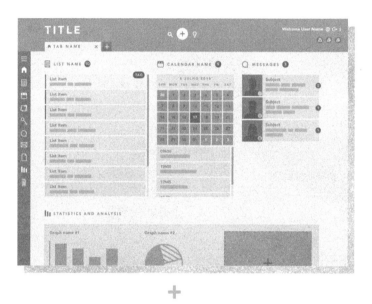

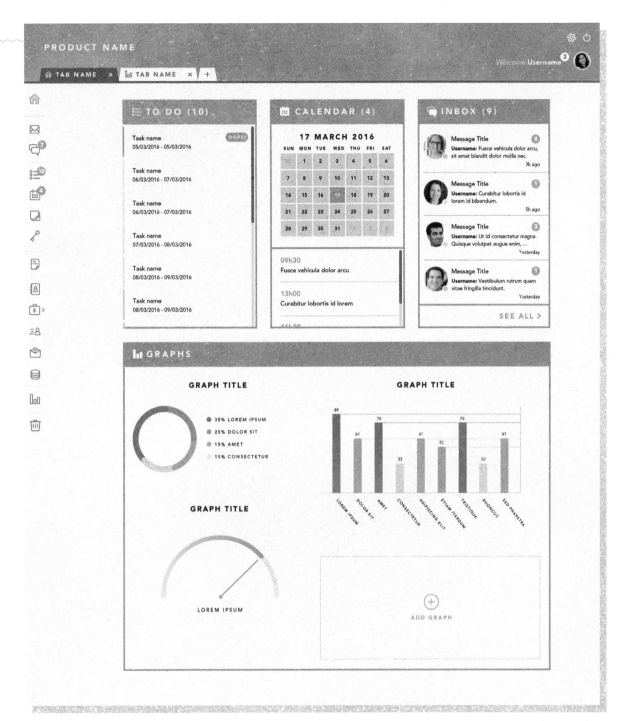

CHAPTER 12

Prototype

The Prototype is the last step of PDP, apart from the High-level Architecture and Project Plan that are done simultaneously and will be covered next. The Prototype is a tool to test and validate the design work that has been done up to this point before advancing to implementation. Ideally, the Prototype should provide a click-through simulation of what the product will look like.

Why

When the design is finished, it is of utmost importance that you ensure that it is properly validated by the product owner. This way, the transition to the most expensive phase – implementation – only happens once you are sure that the product and the design meet expectations. There are, however, two factors that can complicate this step.

The first of these problems is the difficulty of completely comprehending the operation of the user's workflow. When the number of screens is relativity high, it is hard for those that did not develop them and/or are not familiarized with the product's design to understand how the user navigates between them. Simple questions such as how direct links are established between screens could become complex when the design deliveries consist in dozens of screens presented linearly or distributed on a canvas.

The second problem concerns the communication of eventual change requests between product owners and designers. Most design tools do not have satisfactory comment systems and, since they often require paid licenses, product owners will often times not have direct access. To obtain feedback you will have to export the designs to more common formats such as JPG or PDF files. Typically, those files are then, in a best-case scenario, shared in a repository to which the product owner also has access. The product owner then leaves comments on the file or, in a less practical option, sends them by email. In either case, communicating through a single shared file or via files sent by email, giving the fact that those are made on a file that is not directly and automatically synched with the source file, makes it easier for discrepancies to occur between the various design files sent to the product owner.

A clickable Prototype makes the navigation and User Journey easier to understand by offering an experience closer to the real product usage and allows the product owner to validate the design with greater ease and trustworthiness. By making a Prototype with the tools similar to the ones mentioned in the next sections, the product owner can easily leave comments in appropriate places safe in the knowledge that the latest design version is being used.

The Prototype not only makes the communication with the

product owner easier, but also with the development team, where two obstacles usually exist. The first of these is similar to that encountered by the product owner: the developer may have some difficulty comprehending how the product's navigation and user flow work when presented in static pages. The second obstacle concerns the common request from the product owner, independently of how efficient the validation process is, to proceed with changes on the design when the implementation phase has already started. This usually results in discrepancies between the design created and the design implemented and is a consequence of files that are still being used by developers as guides for implementation even after the product owner's requests have rendered them obsolete. The Prototype not only makes the Technical Assessment phase easier, but also guarantees the existence of a master file that is directly synched with the design source files, reducing the chances of discrepancies between design and implementation.

Lastly, the Prototype may also be used to present the product to potential investors (since it allows a richer and more realistic usage experience than static screens), and to carry out early testing with users. The clickable Prototype, however, must only be used for investor or user demonstrations and testing in those cases when the implementation of the first version of the product takes too long (more than three months) or when the product owner needs to gather additional financing for implementation and needs to provide greater assurance about the product concept. The clickable Prototype, given its characteristics explored in the next sections, allows you to obtain feedback regarding the parameters of usefulness and satisfaction defined in the User Research step but provides few insights into efficiency, effectiveness and learnability. Thus, if there are no resources to conduct usability tests in two different iterations, specifically the clickable Prototype and the first prerelease version of the product, we recommend that these tests are completed using the implemented first version.

What

The Prototype constructed in this step is a click-through, which means that it is not a dynamic Prototype and it is not possible to introduce or process any data, but allows the team to simulate navigation from page to page. The execution of this type of Prototype is incredibly fast (it is possible to prototype various user flows in one day) and does not require any code because it can be done using applications such as Marvel App or Invision. These are factors that make this type of prototyping ideal to obtain design validation from the product owner.

112

How

We have already mentioned some of the possible software solutions for this type of Prototype, specifically Marvel App and Invision. Using these tools, the first step is to upload the designs to the chosen application. This can be done by exporting the designed screens to PNG files and thereafter uploading them to the chosen tool or by synching directly the source file to the prototyping application. This second option is recommended, since it provides the previously identified advantages concerning the usage of a single automatically synched file. Once the screens are imported or synched, the next step is to link them in order to represent the user route laid out in the User Journey. To accomplish this, you only need to define the clickable areas in each screen (selecting the desired area with the cursor) and selecting which screen should come next for each area. The objective is not to prototype all the possible interactions in each screen, but to present a realistic use case in a linear fashion. This way there is control over the route that the product owners and developers will take when interacting with the Prototype hence assuring that they see all of the pages.

Examples

Given the interactive nature of this step, it is not possible to provide a proper written example. However, imagine that you are designing an application that facilitates the reservation of tables at restaurants. The Prototype could mirror the following sequence:

Homepage with a clickable area in the search input field > homepage with the search field filled and a clickable area in the button search > results page with a clickable area on a dropdown menu corresponding to an available filter > results page with the previous dropdown menu expanded and with a clickable area on one of the options > results page with the dropdown menu presenting the clicked option and a clickable area on the button filter > results page presenting fewer entries and a clickable area on one of them > page with the details of the selected entry.

This example corresponds to an example of a Prototype that would be used as a base for a more complete analysis of the product's stage.

Further Reading

Handbook of Usability Testing: How to Plan, Design, and Conduct Effective Tests (Jeffrey Rubin and Dana Chisnell, 2008)

113

CHAPTER 13

High-level Architecture

The High-level Architecture (HLA) maps the technical solution of the product under design and should be executed by an experienced software developer working alongside PDP. This will help the designers and the product owner make the best decisions regarding the product itself, as it forces everyone to take into consideration the effort of adding each feature and how these can be shaped to reduce complexity and time to market. HLA is an important step to ensure expectations are realistic and no one is looking to build castles in the sky.

Why

The objective of the HLA step is to provide an overview of how the product is going to be built. This is where you structure the system and identify its constituent components. HLA is where the team determines which of these identified components need to be built and which will be purchased, with which systems the product is going to integrate and how this will happen. It is also during the HLA step that the PDP team baselines the technologies and identifies the skills necessary to build the product. The level of detail should be enough for the tech team that will build the product to understand how to do it, but it should also be general enough to allow some decisions to be taken at the implementation stage as this is when there is more information about the development's progress and the challenges that the development team is facing. This step also baselines the competencies that the development team should have thus providing useful information for the Project Plan.

What

For simple systems, the High-level Architecture can be a one slide diagram stating the main software components and how they interact with each other, like the one in Figure 11.

116

High-level Architecture

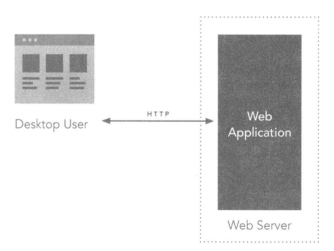

Figure 11/ Sample High-level

For more complex systems, this diagram is just one image among the many pages of a technical architecture document that should cover all the description and responsability for each component, sub-components, and sometimes, sub-sub-components. The complexity level of a technical architecture document should always be driven by the complexity of the product that you are building. And in software, complexity is always driven by the following three aspects of a system:

• Number & size of user interfaces – More user interfaces will result in more web-pages, forms, and select-boxes, for instance, that need to be implemented;

• Complexity of business rules – How much data needs to be captured, quality checked, processed and/or stored? And how many rules or steps does the system need to quality check and process the data? The complexity of the business rules is directly proportional to the amount of data and the number of validation/quality checking and processing steps to operate the data;

• Number & complexity of external systems – Integration with other systems always takes effort because developers need to undersand the data formats and communication flows, translate them all to code, deploy them, and monitor for errors. Furthermore, if and when there are changes to the external systems (either because they were updated or discontinued, for instance), some features might break and you will have to jump into action to fix them. For this reason, the bigger the number of external interfaces the more complex the product will be.

When the complexity forces you to split the system into sub-components, a diagram like the one presented before is not enough to cover all aspects of the system. For these cases, the best way to baseline the architecture is to produce an architecture diagram

117

using a drawing tool or a formal system modeling language like, for example, the Unified Modeling Language (UML)[1]. This general-purpose modeling language is particular to the field of software engineering and was developed to provide a standard way to visualize the design of a system. The language was first released in 1995 with the goal of unifying and standardizing the various notational systems and approaches to software design that had been used up to that time. UML has matured since then and it is now maintained by a not-for-profit entity named the Object Management Group with widespread adoption across the Software Industry where it is used to describe complex systems.

How

The design of the High-level Architecture starts with the Briefing step. Although no decisions will be made at such an early stage of the PDP cycle, it is important to understand the product owner's expectations and how complex the product will be. At this point, you should also take the opportunity to identify opportunities to reduce the complexity of the system you are going to build. Once the Briefing session is over, it is usual to have an idea of the type and size of the product and which technologies you should select for the HLA but in order to ensure that the best decision is made you should also challenge this initial idea constantly throughout PDP. Challenging your original ideas is important because a lot of information will be gathered during the process and sometimes you will discover down the road that there are better tools to get the job done faster.

The architecture will then take shape as the PDP cycle moves forward and, by the time you get to the Execution phase, you need to know which technologies will be used and which components should be built, bought, or integrated. To choose the best technology for a product, several factors should be taken into consideration. Firstly, it is important to choose a technology that already brings considerable value to the table. For example, if you are designing a video game there are already some tools that will speed up the development of this type of digital product. It is always possible to build everything from scratch but employing the reusable components of a video game engine will reduce risk and time-to-market. Similarly, if you are building a news site you should evaluate what is already out there in terms of publishing tools. Probably you can select one and get away with customising a few features. Or it might happen that your news website has many requirements that are unique to its particular case and using a publishing tool would require so many changes that it would be easier to just create a new solution.

For the execise of selecting the best techology for the current product stage, you should assess how each candidate tool fits the purpose of implementing the product requirements. Trade-offs typicaly sacrifice flexibility for reach and a simplistic but useful approach to this challenge is to identify the candidate technology as either a programming language, framework / Software Development Kit (SDK), or as a software product, as depicted in Figure 12.

119

For the execise of selecting the best techology for the current product stage, you should assess how each candidate tool fits the purpose of implementing the product requirements. Trade-offs typicaly sacrifice flexibility for reach and a simplistic but useful approach to this challenge is to identify the candidate technology as either a programming language, framework / Software Development Kit (SDK), or as a software product, as depicted in Figure 12.

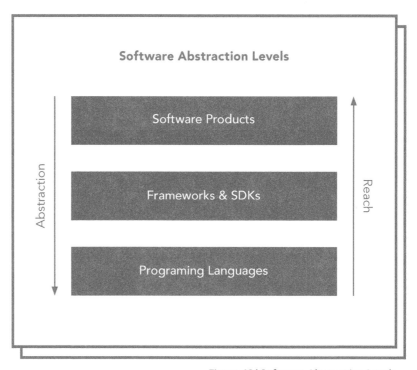

Figure 12/ Software Abstraction Levels

Programming languages provide the highest level of abstraction and it is possible to build any software with just programming languages. That said, this approach could also force you to reinvent the wheel in some cases because some features that are already provided by technologies with lower levels of abstraction are not prebuilt into programming languages. If you were building a house, this would be the sand, water and cement in its foundation.

They are written using a programming language and are dedicated to solving problems in a given domain. There are SDKs for developing mobile applications, frameworks for developing web applications, SDKs for game development, and more. Returning to the house analogy, software frameworks can be seen as the pre-fabricated walls you can buy. But just like pre-fabricated walls, they have their limitations. A pre-fabricated wall that is great for building a home would probably do pretty bad if you were building a prison.

Software products, as the name suggests, are products that can be configured and deployed to deliver your product's goals. Deploying software using a software product should be fast and easy but it provides reduced flexibility. These products are usually built using a framework, but in some cases developers choose to do everything bespoke and use a tool in the programming language layer, instead. The objective of using a software product is to spend as little time coding as possible thus reducing customisation mostly to the configuration of the tool using a visual interface. When this is not enough, software products usually offer a plugin interface that can be used to customise or extend some of the features by developing small software components. Returning once more to the house analogy, software products are akin to buying a pre-built house. You can probably change the collors of

121

walls and make some changes to the lighting or other fittings but it will be quite difficult to add an extra bathroom.

The rule of thumb is to always use the best tool for the job. It is common to use a mix of technologies (and abstraction levels) for highly complex products, especially when you need to break the system into many sub-components. However, keep in mind that in this step you are delivering the High-level Architecture. This step's objective is not to specify and detail each and every sub-component of the system. You should also be aware that the technology with which you are building the product needs to be the best for the current phase of the product. For example, if the goal of the PDP cycle is to build a working product that can be used to test the viability of the business model, you might consider selecting a technology at the software product level to complete a build as quickly as possible. Then, once you have a better understanding of the viability of your product, throw away the first build and do another version aimed at implementing a longer term solution.

Examples

As discussed in the previous section, work on the HLA should start at the Briefing step. As an example, imagine that the product owner wants to build a Customer Relationship Management (CRM) system.

The first question that you need to ask regards the business goals for the current stage of the product. Do you need something to go live fast in order to test the market? Or is the need clearly identified and you are aiming to build a more effective product? This will allow you to clearly identify the level of flexibility needed for each technology. The second question concerns which devices the users possess. Will the users access the web app while working on their desktop or laptop or do they need the application on-the-go as well? The answers to these questions will help you select the correct form-factor, operating system, and technology eco-system for software tools when aiming for lower levels of flexibility but a faster build.

It is healthy to start working on an HLA in the Briefing and witness radical changes happen throughout the PDP cycle. For instance, during the Briefing product owners sometimes state that the product should be available on all devices. If a product owner moots this idea during the Briefing, but the research on the User Research and User Journey steps indicates that the majority of the users will only interact while sitting at their desks, the extra effort of making the application mobile friendly will seem difficult to justify. For this particular CRM system assume that in the early stages of the product users will be sitting at their desks most of the time but you also need to support a couple of on-the-go features. The team has also determined that this first version will be used to test the market but found it more feasible to deliver a smaller product with a proven technology than one with many features in a technology that would require a complete re-build later down the road.

After analysing the several options and looking at the abstraction layers on Figure 13, presented earlier, the team realizes that it is better to work with technologies at the framework and SDK level for two reasons. Firstly, because there are good frameworks for web applications that already solve many issues specific to this domain. Secondly, because some of the features are specific to this product (like some operations that should be available in mobile while others should not), thus using something at the software product layer would require many changes

123

that force the developers to spend considerable time circumventing the limitations of the techology. After several iterations during the PDP, the final architecture can be found in Figure 13.

CRM High-level Architecture

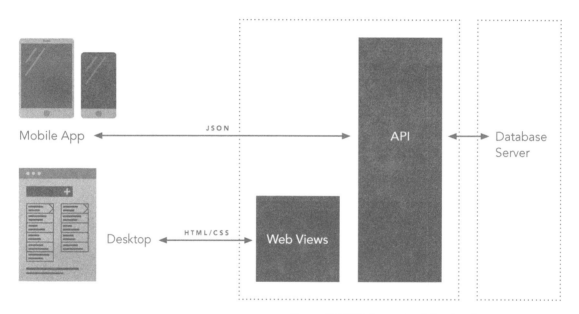

Figure 13/ CRM System High-level Architecture

The left side of the figure shows how users will interact with the application. The user can access all of the product's features through the web-browser on their computer but also has quick access to a few key features on their mobile devices through an app. On the center of Figure 13 you can see that the web application will be installed on a web server and there will be an API (Application Programming Interface) to serve the mobile application. On the right side you can see that the data will be stored in a database on a separate server.

References

1. The Unified Modeling Language User Guide (Grady Booch, 1998)

Fowler, M. (2003). UML Distilled: A Brief Guide to the Standard

Further Reading

Object Modeling Language (3rd ed.). Addison-Wesley Professional.

Fowler, M. (2002). Patterns of Enterprise Application Architecture.

Addison-Wesley Professional.

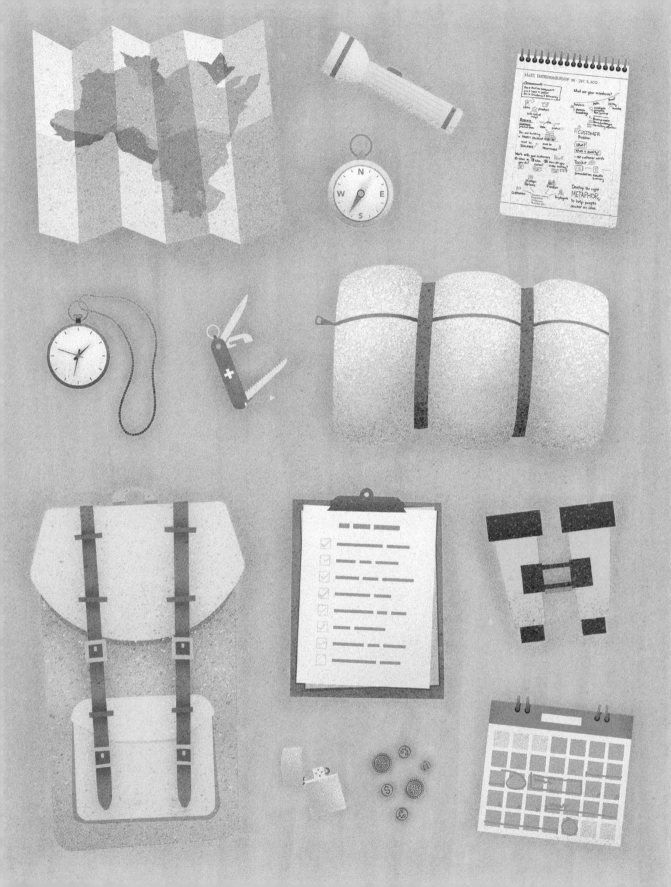

CHAPTER 14

Project Plan

The Project Plan is the link between the design and the development stages of any software product. This is where we detail the steps to build the project, what resources are needed and when delivery will occur.

Why

The Project Plan is an important step in any project. Even when you are dealing with Agile projects there is still some planning involved and it should not be seen as a tool exclusive to Waterfall projects. Plans can be laid out at a higher level where they are usually broken into phases of weeks or even months or they can focus on the short-term where a team details which tasks are going to be addressed in the upcoming days or weeks and leaves the remaining work to be detailed on a later stage. Contrary to popular belief, plans should be living documents and reviewed on a regular basis.

What

For a short-term plan (one where delivery is weeks away) it is common to use a simple spreadsheet containing a list of well-defined tasks or user stories, estimates - in hours - and a column containing the tasks' statuses (not started, in progress, in review, etc). For medium term projects (projects where timelines are months away), you can use a project planning tool or a more elaborate spreadsheet. As with projects that will only cover a few weeks, it will be useful to group tasks by categories, often called work packages or epics. For long-term projects (those with a duration ranging from months to years), spreadsheets can be used as intermediate planning tools but the end document will need to cover the scope of the project at a very high level that is usually broken into phases. The final document should be a presentation or a few pages that allow the plan to be shared and discussed with anyone in the team as well as external stakeholders.

As stated above, depending on the project, you might want to plan it in phases, work-packages, tasks, epics, or user-stories just to name a few organizing units. The scope of this book is not to force on the reader a particular approach to Project Planning so we will simply refer to these hereafter as units of work. The goal is to ensure that there is a plan to be discussed and built upon. Disregarding which unit of work and which type of planning (short-term, mid-term, or long-term), you will need to ensure that the following aspects are covered:

Scope	What needs to be achieved, which consist of the requirements that were broken into units of work.
Time	When will all units of work be completed, taking into account the dependencies between them (for example, to implement a user dashboard feature the system needs to have already implemented some features regarding user accounts and displayed data).
Costs	How much it will cost, either in terms of currency, effort, or complexity. Some Agile methodologies avoid using specific measures, like hours or currency and prefer to use the relative complexity between units of work as a measure often called story points.
Quality	Defines the error tolerance for a given product stage. Higher quality means greater costs and a longer schedule. For example, an application that publishes news on the web can be more tolerant to errors (i.e. bugs) than a product aiding a medical team in an operating theater.

129

Table 12/ Definition of Scope, Time, Costs and Quality

The four aspects mentioned should be enough to define every aspect of the project and a change in one will impact the others. The relation between these aspects is often depicted as a triangle, like the one presented in Figure 14, and are often called the four dimensions of a Project Plan.

Figure 14/ The four dimentions of a Project Plan

How

Although this step should start as soon as possible, the majority of its development happens when the other steps are complete with the exception of the Prototype step. And although all steps generate input, the Decision Matrix is often the starting point because it already states all of the features and their priority.

A functional plan should also include a few tasks not usually considered on the Decision Matrix but that need to be completed as part of the project. For example, developers will need to setup their environment, their development process (code storage system, continuous integration service, etc) and quality assurance will also need to be planned (e.g. quality checkpoints, regression tests, etc). You should also consider the budgeted effort for additional design as not all screens will be laid out during PDP and some will require changes during the implementation of the product as the team receives additional feedback during the product's implementation. Some teams also budget effort for project management and communication (often 20% of total effort but this can be less for simple projects with senior teams or more for products of great complexity). We consider planning and budgeting in effort for project management to be a good practice and it should happen on every project. The main difference between Waterfall and Agile projects is that during the former most of the project management effort will be executed by a project manager while during the latter this effort will be distributed across the team.

Once everything that needs to be done has been compiled into a list, the way the plan is developed depends on the methodology that the project team will use to implement the product. We are going to provide an overview for both Waterfall and Agile projects but PDP does not encourage the usage of a specific practice. As a result we will not be providing a high degree of detail for each one so if you want to know more about them please refer to the further reading section at the end of this chapter.

Examples

If the team that will develop the product is using an Agile approach, the Project Planning step should be easy to complete. Agile methodologies promote continuous learning and regular iterations of the product throughout the development and project planning processes. The best way forward is to plan a sprint that covers all of the setup tasks (i.e. bringing the team together, setting up the deployment procedure, setting up development, testing and production environments, etc), plus several additional sprints to cover the features that should be tackled first. The effort for these units of work should be estimated by the team according to the vision discussed with the product owner to ensure that they are aligned with expectations.

For development teams using a Waterfall methodology, the Project Plan will take a bit more effort to complete because this methodology promotes planning ahead and, in most cases, the risks of the project are identified and the respective mitigations are planned and corrected earlier in the process. This means that for this approach planning a few weeks ahead is not enough and the PDP plan needs to cover, at a minimum, all high priority features. We often dedicate phase 1 to the development of all higher priority features. Sometimes product owners need to get buy in for the entire product and teams might be asked to develop a Project Plan for all of the possible features. However, planning a second phase in detail is difficult, as the team will need to base their decisions on reasonable assumptions and, in most cases, planning phase 2 ahead introduces levels of risk that are difficult to manage. Nevertheless, an experienced team with good processes might enjoy success with this level of planning and creating a plan for the full feature set could be a viable option.

Further Reading

Agile Estimating and Planning (Mike Cohn, 2005)

A Guide to the Project Management Body of Knowledge (PMI, 2017)

Agile Practice Guide (PMI, 2017)

CHAPTER 15

Conclusion

In 1820 André-Marie Ampère published the Biot-Savart Law and founded what is known as electrodynamics – a new branch of physics that deals with the changes of electric and magnetic fields. Those were exciting times, and the number of physicists publishing new discoveries in that area in the upcoming years exploded. But although progress was good in the academia, the amount of equations and models related to electromagnetism was massive, and operating in the field was a nightmare. Four decades later, James Clerk Maxwell dedicated his career to solving this issue. Between 1861 and 1862, he published a four part paper in which he summarized a big portion of the knowledge in electromagnetism in only four equations. Understanding the equations required knowledge of advanced calculus, but it was a basic requirement for someone researching or developing products in the fields of electronics, electricity or electromagnetism. Although his work delivered great progress, compiling and simplifying information in a knowledge area is not always recognized in the same proportion of the value that it delivers. It is always easy to spot and recognize someone that discovers something new, but it's hard to find value in someone's work for compiling and organizing something that is already known. Despite the fast moving pace of electrodynamics in the 19th century, it took 27 years for Maxwell's work to be widely adopted, and it was Albert Einstein himself who popularized the name "Maxwell's Equations" - delivering to its author the recognition he deserved.

Fast forward to today and looking at our particular case. A decade spent developing digital products as turned out to be a great teacher, allowing us to take a deep dive into almost every known UX/UI technique, and select the ones that make sense as a whole. The Product Design Process should be seen as Maxwell's Equations for designing digital products. A compilation and simplification of a huge knowledge area, allowing people to master it without the need to navigate through a great number of books, papers and perspectives.

Each step of PDP consists on a widely adopted technique. It was not our goal to develop or introduce new ways of gathering user requirements, developing graphic interfaces or designing software systems. Our objective was to understand which techniques are relevant as a whole and how the output of one can contribute to the following steps of a design process. The curation and mapping of these techniques is where the gold can be found, as the ones that we selected serve a specific purpose in the design process. The information that each step produces is relevant to other steps down the line, as shown in Figure 15, at the end of this last chapter. For example, the User Research step helps us identify products used by the target users, which in turn is relevant to the Benchmark – allowing us to identify where we should look for features and UX references. But a successful User Research can only be done with a targeted market segment, which is gathered in the Briefing.

This manual was though and developed with the purpose of making the design process accessible to anyone with basic knowledge of product design or development. It should give them a process to follow on their own projects and improve the results. Nevertheless, being an expert on UX, UI or software development helps the understanding of the concepts covered in this manual. However, less experienced professionals should also find in this book a good way to start.

We are aware that product design is not an area in which someone can provide a definitive solution and guarantee the success of every digital product. Mainly because success and failure are not determined solely by how successfully a product meets its goals. In a product lifecycle, success and failure also depend on the sustainability of the company that owns the product, stability of its team and even external political factors – just to name a few variables outside the product design realm that can dictate the success or failure of a product. Despite all these, mastering the product design stage and delivering a beautiful product that perfectly meets the user and business goals, is one problem that you should now be able to scratch of the list.

137

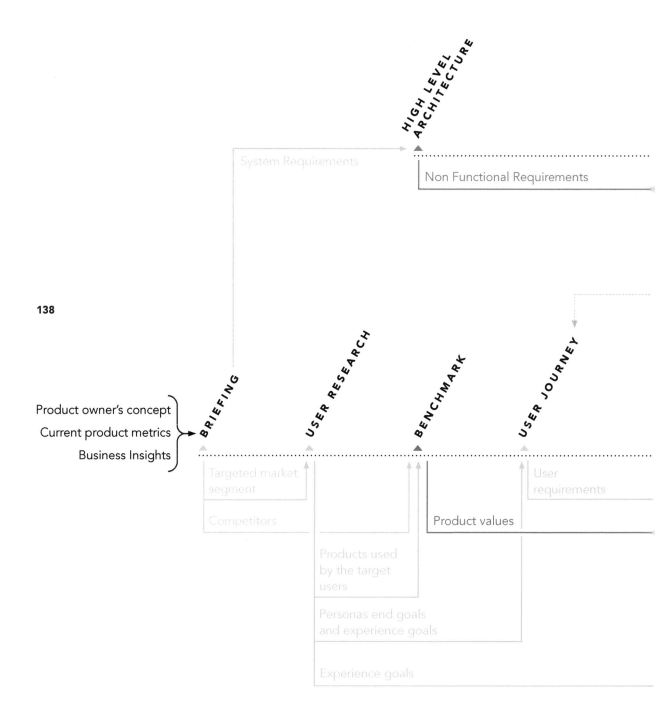

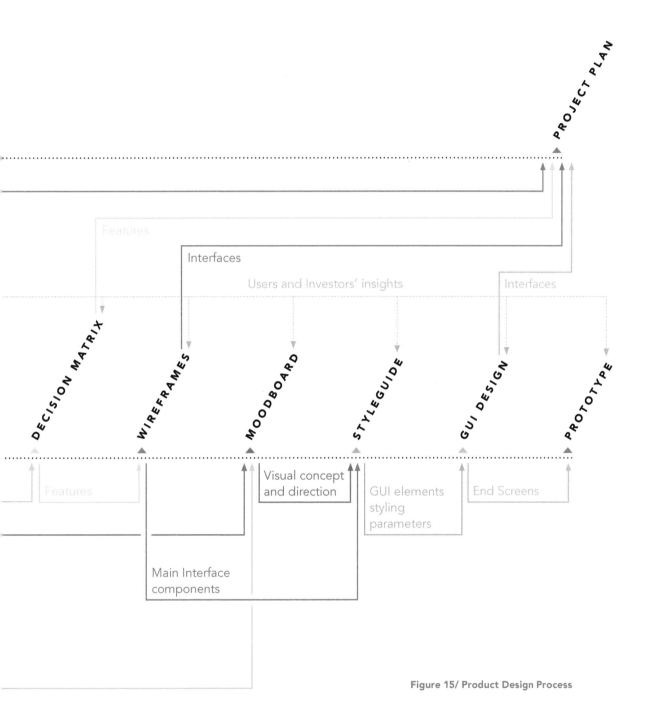

PROJECT PLAN

Features

Interfaces

Users and Investors' insights

Interfaces

DECISION MATRIX

WIREFRAMES

MOODBOARD

STYLEGUIDE

GUI DESIGN

PROTOTYPE

Features

Visual concept and direction

GUI elements styling parameters

End Screens

Main Interface components

Figure 15/ Product Design Process

CPSIA information can be obtained
at www.ICGtesting.com
Printed in the USA
BVHW020952171121
621844BV00017B/486